Around the World
VEGETARIAN
COOKBOOK

MARY BAYRAMIAN

ILLUSTRATED BY PATRICIA KINLEY

TROUBADOR PRESS SAN FRANCISCO

In Dedication

To our Armenian mama who inspired
us to prepare food with love, creativ-
ity and imagination.

Published in the United States of America by
TROUBADOR PRESS
385 Fremont Street
San Francisco, California 94105

Library of Congress Cataloging in Publication Data

Bayramian, Mary, 1921–
    Around the world vegetarian cookbook.

    1. Vegetarianism.   2. Cookery, International.
I. Title.   II. Title: Vegetarian cookbook.
TX837.B36   641.5′636   76–18736
ISBN 0–912300–68–X
ISBN 0–912300–67–1 pbk.

Contents

ACKNOWLEDGMENT

We want to express appreciation to our many friends who so kindly contributed their favorite ethnic vegetarian recipes. Most of all to the mothers of all countries, generations past, who with patience and love taught their daughters the art of cooking . . . to them our deep-felt thanks.

Approximate Equivalent Measures

U.S.	Metric
1 quart (32 fl. oz.)	9.5 decilitres
1 pint (16 fl. oz.)	4.7 decilitres
1 cup (8 fl. oz.)	2.4 decilitres
1 tablespoon (1/3 fl. oz.)	1.5 centilitres
1 teaspoon (1/9 fl. oz.)	.5 centilitres
1 pound (16 oz.)	approximately 500 grams
1/2 pound (8 oz.)	approximately 250 grams
1/4 pound (4 oz.)	approximately 120 grams
(1 oz.)	approximately 30 grams

Introduction

Cooking is primarily an art. Food can be wholesome as well as delicious. It is an art when one can combine the good things of the earth to bring out the ultimate in flavor. Food prepared with a light heart and in a happy frame of mind is often the best food. Preparing the special foods that are favorites of those you love . . . searching for new foods, reflect your care.

The recipes included are both simple and sophisticated, elegant and easy to prepare, enabling one to duplicate the dishes which have become famous around the world among gourmets, chefs and every lover of the exquisite in food. The secret lies in the artful use of herbs and flavorings, in unusual combinations, and in the addition of various ingredients at different times to create perfect blending. The recipes were carefully selected from food enjoyed around the world and can be easily and readily prepared with ingredients from home gardens, health food stores and supermarket shelves. Many of the recipes are one-meal dishes, a delight when one is limited in preparation time.

We hope you find great pleasure in eating the foods from around the world; that you will use the recipes in this collection freely and frequently to add new and exciting dishes to your cookery repertoire.

African

Since the Northern region of Africa has a more Mideastern style of cooking, it is below the Sahara that one finds a distinctive African cuisine. Deep in the African bush, the farmer often lives on milk, curds and whey, beans and cereals, and green vegetables. For nourishing bulk they use starchy tubers like the cassava, yam and sweet potato. Especially along the West coast of Africa, the yam has helped the people to survive. In Ghana, the Ashanti celebrate feast days with a variety of yam dishes. These figure in the ceremonies that solemnize birth, death and marriage. The yam is often accompanied by an egg sauce, because the egg has been an immemorial symbol of fertility and triumph. Africans have a special fondness for ostrich eggs; a single egg weighs about three pounds and will feed a dozen people. Ferociously hot chili peppers are used in one form or another, in much of African cooking. Interestingly, chilies in food tend to stimulate the appetite and cool the body temperature. A soothing complement to the fiery spices of the food is provided by bread made of millet, called *injera*. Thin and round like a giant pancake, it has a unique faintly sour flavor. On the Eastern coast of the continent, an unusual diet has been inspired by the strict religious customs of the Ethiopians, who are expected to fast as many as 200 days of the year. A day of fast requires complete abstinence until midday, and then only allows such foods as cereals, beans, and lentils. The rigors of this fasting have induced the Ethiopians to invent vegetable substitutes for meat as no other culture in Africa has done.

ETHIOPIAN YEMISER SELATTA
Lentil, shallot and chili salad

1 ¼ cups brown lentils
3 tablespoons red wine vinegar
2 tablespoons oil
1 teaspoon salt
freshly ground black pepper

6 large shallot cloves, peeled and cut in halves
2 fresh hot chilies, seeded and slivered in strips

Wash lentils and drain in a sieve. Place lentils in a saucepan and add water to cover them by 2 inches. Bring to a quick boil; reduce the heat to low. Cover the pan partially and simmer until the lentils are tender but still somewhat firm to the bite, about 20 minutes. Drain the lentils in a sieve or colander and rinse them under cold running water to cool them quickly; drain thoroughly. In a serving bowl, combine the vinegar, oil, salt and a few grindings of pepper; beat them together with a whisk. Add lentils, shallots and chilies; gently mix thoroughly with a fork. Taste for seasoning and let the salad marinate at room temperature for at least an hour, stirring gently from time to time. Serves four.

WEST AFRICAN SLAAI
Avocado, peanut and ginger salad

2 tablespoons lemon juice
1 teaspoon ginger
1 teaspoon salt

2 large ripe avocados, cut in ½-inch cubes
½ cup peanuts, coarsely chopped

In a serving bowl, combine the lemon juice, ginger and salt, stir until well mixed. Add avocado cubes and toss gently and thoroughly. Let the salad marinate at room temperature for at least 30 minutes and sprinkle with chopped peanuts. Serves four.

WEST AFRICAN GEELRYS
Rice with raisins

2 tablespoons butter
1 cup uncooked long-grain rice
2 cups water
1 piece of stick cinnamon, 2 inches long
½ teaspoon ground turmeric
pinch of saffron threads, crumbled

1 teaspoon salt
½ cup seedless raisins
1 teaspoon sugar

In a heavy saucepan, melt the butter over moderate heat, add the rice and stir until the grains are coated with butter. Do not let the rice brown. Add the water, cinnamon, turmeric, saffron and salt. Stirring constantly, bring to a boil over high heat. Reduce the heat to low, cover tightly and simmer for 20 minutes, or until the rice is tender and has absorbed all the liquid in the pan. Remove the pan from the heat, discard the cinnamon stick and add the raisins. Gently fluff the rice with a fork, stir in sugar, taste and add more if you wish. Cover the pan with its lid and let stand at room temperature for about 20 minutes. Just before serving, fluff the rice again with a fork and mound it in a heated bowl. Serves four.

WEST AFRICAN PAPAIA
Papaya and chili relish

1 ripe papaya, about 1 pound
1 tablespoon lemon juice

1 tablespoon fresh hot chilies, seeded
and minced

Peel, seed and cut papaya into ½-inch cubes. In a serving bowl, combine the papaya, lemon juice and chilies. Toss the mixture together gently but thoroughly. Cover tightly and let the mixture marinate at room temperature for about 2 hours before serving. Serves four.

ETHIOPIA YATAKETE KILKIL
Vegetables with ginger and garlic

8 small boiling potatoes
3 large carrots, peeled, cut lengthwise into quarters and then crosswise in 2-inch lengths
½ pound fresh green beans, cut in 2-inch lengths
4 tablespoons vegetable oil
2 onions, quartered and cut in 1/2-inch slices

1 large green pepper, cut in strips
2 whole fresh hot chilies, finely chopped
1 tablespoon garlic, finely chopped
2 teaspoons fresh ginger root, finely chopped
1 teaspoon salt
½ teaspoon white pepper
6 green onions, cut in 2-inch lengths including green tops

Peel the potatoes, then with a small sharp knife, cut out narrow V-shaped wedges ¼-inch deep at ½-inch intervals all around the length of the potatoes. In a large kettle, boil lightly salted water and drop in potatoes, carrots and string beans, let the vegetables boil briskly, uncovered, for 5 minutes. Drain in a colander and run cold water over them to stop their cooking. In a heavy large casserole, heat the oil until hot and add the onions, green peppers and chilies, stirring frequently and cook for about 5 minutes or until vegetables are soft but not brown. Add the garlic, ginger, salt and pepper, and stir for a few minutes. Add the potatoes, carrots, string beans and the green onions to the casserole. Stir until vegetables are coated with the oil mixture. Reduce the heat to low and cook for about 10 minutes or until the vegetables are tender but still somewhat crisp. Serve immediately. Serves four.

MOZAMBIQUE ARROZ DE COCO
Rice with tomatoes, chilies and coconut

1 cup fresh coconut, peeled and chopped
1½ cups hot water
2 tablespoons oil
½ cup onion, finely chopped
1 small bell pepper, finely chopped

1 cup uncooked rice
2 tomatoes, peeled and finely chopped
1 teaspoon salt
2 teaspoons fresh hot chilies, finely minced

In a blender combine coconut and hot water; blend till smooth. In a heavy skillet, heat the oil, add onion and bell pepper. Stirring frequently, cook until they are soft but not brown. Add the rice and stir for a few minutes until the grains are evenly coated. Stir in the coconut liquid, tomatoes, salt and bring to a simmer over moderate heat. Cover the pan tightly, reduce the heat to its lowest point and simmer for about 20 minutes or until all the liquid has been absorbed. Remove the pan from the heat, stir in the chilies and taste for seasoning. Cover again and let the rice rest at room temperature for about 10 minutes before serving. When ready, fluff rice gently with a fork and place in a heated bowl. Serves four.

SOUTH AFRICAN ATJAR
Cucumber and hot chilies salad

2 large cucumbers
3 tablespoons red wine vinegar
½ teaspoon sugar
1½ teaspoons salt

1 teaspoon oil
2 teaspoons fresh hot chilies, finely chopped

Peel cucumbers and slice into ⅛-inch thick slices. In a bowl mix 1 tablespoon of the vinegar and ¼ teaspoon of sugar and all of the salt. Mix thoroughly, add cucumbers and mix well. Let cucumbers marinate at room temperature for about half an hour, then squeeze the slices vigorously to remove moisture; place in a serving bowl. Add the remaining 2 tablespoons of vinegar, ¼ teaspoon of sugar and the chilies. Toss together gently but thoroughly; serve at once. Serves four.

11

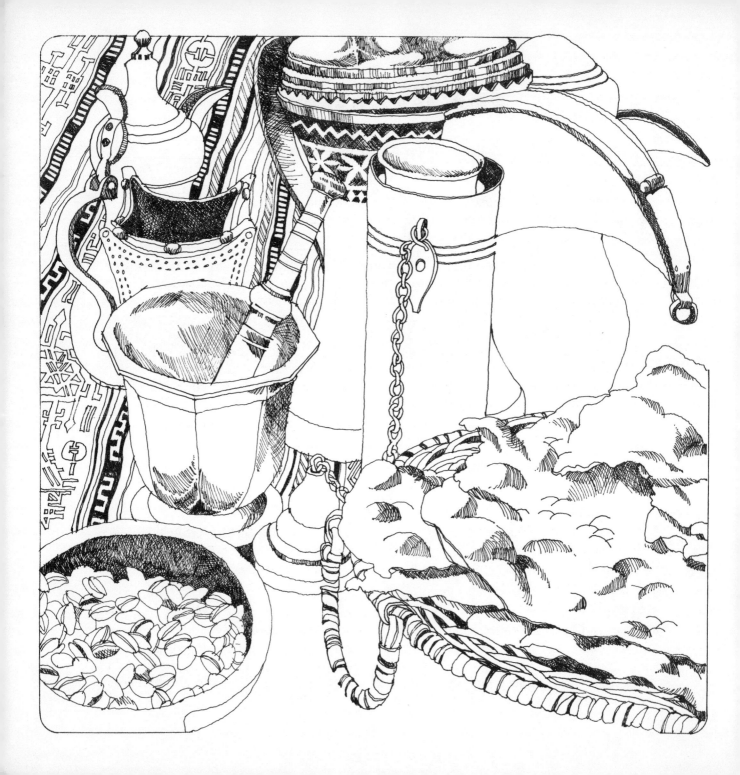

Armenian

In Armenian cooking, as in most preparations from the Mediterranean and Middle East, one finds traditionally prevalent use of tomato, green pepper, eggplant, garlic and onions, which are combined with aromatic herbs and spices. But the heart and soul of Armenian cooking is based on bulgur, a cracked wheat. Bulgur is processed by boiling the whole wheat until the grains puff to three times their size. The cooked wheat is then spread on screens to cure in the sun. The dried grain, crisp and brown, is hulled and then ground into three different sizes—fine, medium and coarse. Bulgur is considered the staff of life in the Armenian pantry. Unique in flavor, it nutritiously enhances Armenian foods, and can be deliciously prepared in a multitude of ways. Another important food for the Armenian people is yogurt, which they believe to be the supreme health food, conferring long life, prolonging youth and fortifying the soul. Even today, Armenians make their yogurt at home, fermenting it with a starter saved from the previous batch. It is delicious plain, or can be diluted half and half with water and a few ice cubes, quenching thirst better than carbonated soft drinks. In summer it makes a cooling salad with cucumbers and mint, and in winter, enhances hot thick soups. So great was this attachment to yogurt that many years ago the housewife, preparing to emigrate to a foreign land, spread a cloth with yogurt, let it dry and packed it among her indispensable possessions as a starter for her new home.

ARMENIAN

VOSBOV KUFTE
Lentils and bulgur, with parsley and butter

1 cup pink lentils
2½ cups water
⅓ cup onion, finely diced
¾ cup butter
1¼ cups fine bulgur
1½ teaspoons salt

1 teaspoon coarse ground red pepper
¼ cup green onion, finely sliced
¼ cup parsley, finely chopped
¼ cup green pepper, finely diced
sprigs of parsley
sprinkling of paprika

In a saucepan bring to boil lentils and water, and continue cooking until lentils are soft, about 25 minutes. In another saucepan sauté onion in butter for about 5 minutes. In a large bowl place bulgur, lentil mixture (hot), salt and red pepper. Mix well—about 3 or 4 minutes—add butter and onion mixture and knead another minute. Add mixture of green onion, parsley and green pepper. Taste for seasoning and add more salt if necessary. Spoon on platter and garnish with sprigs of parsley and a sprinkling of paprika; serve hot immediately. Serves four.

VAROONK AGHTZAN
Cucumber, yogurt and mint salad

2½ cups cucumbers, peeled and diced
2 cups yogurt
2 teaspoons dried mint leaves, crushed

1 teaspoon salt
1 small clove garlic, finely chopped

In a bowl mix all ingredients thoroughly. Chill in refrigerator until serving time. Spoon into four individual salad bowls. Most refreshing on a hot summer day. Serves four.

BULGUR AGHTZAN
Cracked wheat, tomato and cucumber salad

2 cups water
1 cup bulgur
1 cucumber, pared and cut in ½-inch
  cubes
1 tomato, cut in ½-inch cubes
1 green bell pepper, cut in ½-inch cubes
1 bunch green onions, trimmed and cut
  in ¼-inch slices

¼ cup parsley, finely chopped
2 teaspoons salt
½ teaspoon black pepper
3 tablespoons lemon juice
¼ cup olive oil

Bring the water to a boil in a 2-quart saucepan and slowly pour in bulgur. Cover the pan, lower the heat and simmer for 10 minutes or until all the water has been absorbed. Uncover the pan and, stirring frequently, cook over low heat for another few minutes to dry the grains. Spoon into a large bowl and cool to room temperature; then cover and refrigerate for at least 30 minutes until thoroughly chilled. Add the cucumber, tomato, green pepper, onions and parsley to the chilled bulgur. Season with salt and pepper. Just before serving, sprinkle the salad with lemon juice and pour in olive oil. Toss the salad together lightly but thoroughly and taste for seasoning. Serve on a platter and decorate with sprigs of parsley. Serves four generously.

LOLIG AGHTZAN
Tomato salad

4 tomatoes, chopped
1 small green pepper, finely chopped
¼ cup parsley, finely chopped
¼ cup green onions, finely sliced

2 tablespoons lemon juice
1 teaspoon salt
¼ teaspoon coarse red pepper

Mix together all ingredients in a glass or ceramic bowl. Chill for 30 minutes before serving. Serves four.

This is a traditional salad served with most Armenian recipes. Delicious and very refreshing.

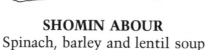

SHOMIN ABOUR
Spinach, barley and lentil soup

1 quart water
½ cup barley
1 bunch spinach, washed and chopped
½ cup lentils
1 clove garlic, minced
salt to taste

⅓ cup tomato paste
2 cups strained canned tomatoes
2 tablespoons lemon juice
1 tablespoon dried mint leaves, crushed

Bring to a boil in one quart of water: barley, spinach, lentils and garlic. Simmer for 25 minutes. Add salt, tomato paste, tomatoes and lemon juice. Simmer for another 25 minutes or until barley is soft. Stir in mint. Serve very hot. Serves four.

HOMMUS
Garbanzo bean dip

nned garbanzos
poons toasted sesame seeds
spoons olive oil
espoons lemon juice
ge clove garlic

¼ teaspoon ground cumin
salt and pepper
chopped parsley
peda bread wedges (see page 19)

Drain and save liquid from garbanzos. In blender, place garbanzos, sesame seeds, olive oil, lemon juice, garlic and cumin. Pour in ¼ cup of garbanzo liquid and blend—starting and stopping motor to add more liquid if needed—until smooth and the consistency of heavy batter. Season with salt and pepper. Spoon into a bowl and garnish with chopped parsley. Excellent served with peda bread wedges. Makes about 1½ cups.

DAEDZADZ TANABOUR
Barley and yogurt soup

⅔ cup barley
4 cups water
salt to taste
4 cups yogurt

1 egg
1½ tablespoons mint leaves, dried and crushed
¼ cup butter

Simmer barley in water for 1½ hours or until barley is tender. Add salt. In a bowl beat thoroughly yogurt and egg. Pour some of the cooked barley mixture slowly into yogurt mixture stirring constantly. Blend the remaining two mixtures together and stir in mint. Melt butter in a saucepan and pour over soup. Serve very hot. Serves four.

LOUPIA AGHTZAN
Black-eyed bean salad

2 cups black-eyed beans
2 cups water
¼ cup parsley, finely chopped
¼ cup onion, finely chopped

2 tablespoons green pepper, chopped
2 tablespoons lemon juice
salt and hot cayenne pepper to taste

In a covered saucepan boil black-eyed beans in water for about 30 minutes or until beans are tender but firm. Drain and cool. In a salad bowl add to cooled beans: parsley, onion and green pepper. Sprinkle with lemon juice and toss thoroughly. Season with salt and cayenne pepper to taste. Chill until ready to serve. Serves four.

DABGODZ SEMPOOG
Fried eggplant sandwiches

4 eggs
3 tablespoons flour
¼ teaspoon salt
¾ cup oil
1 large eggplant, sliced lengthwise ¼-inch thick

4 tomatoes, sliced
1 green pepper, sliced in rings
1 cucumber, thinly sliced
1 onion, thinly sliced
¼ cup parsley, finely chopped
assorted breads

Beat together in a bowl: eggs, flour and salt. Heat shortening in a 9-inch frying pan. Dip eggplant slices in egg mixture and place in frying pan as many slices as cover the bottom of the pan. Fry until golden brown on each side. To serve, arrange eggplant slices in center of large platter, surround with tomatoes, pepper rings, cucumber slices, onion slices and sprinkle with chopped parsley. Serve either hot or cold with assorted breads. Serves four.

PEDA HATZ
Armenian yeast bread

½ cup lukewarm water
2 packages active dry yeast
8 teaspoons sugar
6 cups flour
1 tablespoon salt
1¾ cups lukewarm milk

4 tablespoons olive oil
2 tablespoons soft butter
1 egg yolk, mixed with 1 tablespoon water
4 tablespoons sesame seeds

In a small bowl pour in lukewarm water, sprinkle in yeast and 2 teaspoons of the sugar. Let mixture rest for a few minutes, then stir to dissolve the yeast. Set the bowl in a warm place for about 10 minutes. Place 5½ cups of the flour in a deep mixing bowl and add the remaining 6 teaspoons of sugar and the salt. Make a well in the center and pour in the yeast mixture, lukewarm milk and 3 tablespoons of the olive oil. With a large wooden spoon, gradually mix and stir until the dough can be gathered into a ball. Place the dough on a surface sprinkled with the remaining ½ cup of flour and knead, pushing the dough down with the heels of your hands, pressing it forward and folding it back on itself. When the dough is smooth and elastic, cut in half. Spread the butter on two baking sheets. With your hands, flatten the two balls of dough into round cakes each 1½ inches thick and about 8 inches in diameter. Place them on the baking sheets. Brush the surface with the remaining tablespoon of olive oil, cover lightly with a kitchen towel and set aside in a draft-free place for about 1 hour, or until the dough has doubled in volume. Preheat oven to 350 degrees. With a pastry brush, coat the surface of the loaves with the egg-yolk-and-water mixture and sprinkle with the sesame seeds. Make a dimple in center of each loaf with forefinger, and two more dimples on each quarter like a cross. Bake in the center of the oven for 30 minutes, then transfer the loaves to wire racks to cool before serving. Makes 2 loaves.

TZITAYOUGH SEMPOOG
Eggplant with tomatoes and green peppers

1 cup tomato sauce
⅔ cup olive oil
¼ cup parsley, chopped
1 teaspoon salt
½ teaspoon black pepper
½ teaspoon coarse ground red pepper
½ teaspoon allspice

½ cup celery, thinly sliced
1 large eggplant, cut into 1-inch squares
3 tomatoes, cut into ¾-inch squares
2 onions, thinly sliced
1 large green pepper, cut into ¾-inch squares

In a small bowl mix tomato sauce, olive oil, parsley, salt, pepper, red pepper, allspice and celery. In a 12 × 7 × 2-inch pan spread half of eggplant, and over this: half of tomatoes, onions, green pepper and half of prepared tomato sauce mixture. Arrange remaining eggplant and remaining vegetables and cover with remaining tomato sauce mixture. Bake in a 400-degree oven covered for 30 minutes and remove cover for another 30 minutes of baking. Delicious hot or cold. Serves four.

LOLIG AGHTZAN SEMPOOG
Eggplant and tomato salad

1 eggplant, cut in ¾-inch cubes
3 tablespoons butter
4 tomatoes, diced
1 green pepper, diced

¼ cup parsley, finely chopped
¼ cup green onions, finely sliced
2 tablespoons lemon juice
salt and cayenne pepper to taste

Sauté cubed eggplant in butter in a covered saucepan for about 15 minutes or until eggplant is soft, stirring occasionally. Do not burn and if necessary add 1 tablespoon water during cooking. Chill mixture. In a glass or ceramic salad bowl, combine chilled eggplant, tomatoes, green pepper, parsley, onions, lemon juice, salt and dash of cayenne pepper. Toss thoroughly and adjust seasoning if necessary. Serves four.

GARAK YOOGHOV KUFTE
Bulgur, with tomatoes and green pepper

2 cups fine bulgur
3 tablespoons tomato paste
⅓ cup hot water
1 onion, finely diced
¾ cup butter or olive oil

4 tomatoes, diced
1 green pepper, finely diced
1½ teaspoons salt
1 teaspoon coarse ground red pepper

Place bulgur in mixing bowl. Dissolve tomato paste in hot water and mix into bulgur. In a saucepan sauté onions in butter or olive oil for a few minutes. Add tomatoes and green peppers; sauté for 5 minutes. Pour tomato mixture on bulgur and add salt and red pepper. Knead with hands until well blended. Spoon on serving platter, smooth surface with hand dipped in water. Serve while it is still warm. Serves four.

BOODOUK PIAZE
Olive and nut salad

2½ cups pitted green or black olives, cut
   in half
⅓ cup onion, finely chopped
⅓ cup parsley, finely chopped
⅓ cup walnuts, coarsely chopped

⅓ cup tomato paste
2 tablespoons lemon juice
salt to taste
dash of cayenne pepper
2 tomatoes, cut in wedges

In a bowl combine olives, onions, parsley and walnuts. In another small bowl mix tomato paste, lemon juice, salt and dash of cayenne pepper. Pour over olive mixture and toss thoroughly. Chill for at least one hour. Spoon into four individual salad bowls and garnish with tomato wedges. Serves four.

VOSBOV PILAV
Lentil and bulgar pilaf

1 cup brown lentils
3 cups water
1 cup coarse bulgur

salt and pepper to taste
1 medium onion, finely chopped
½ cup butter

Place in a two-quart saucepan: lentils and water. Bring to a boil and simmer for 20 minutes or until lentils are firm but tender. Add bulgur and salt and bring to boil. Simmer for about 15 minutes or until bulgur is cooked and the water is absorbed. In a small saucepan sauté butter and onions until golden; add to lentil and bulgur mixture. Cover and let stand for 5 minutes. Sprinkle with black pepper and serve warm. Serves four.

CHIR ASHI
Apricot, garbanzo bean and lentil stew

1½ cups dried apricots, soaked in 1½ cups water for 1 hour
½ cup garbanzo beans, covered with water and soaked overnight

1 cup lentils
2 cups onions, sliced
⅓ cup honey
2 teaspoons salt

In a large saucepan bring apricots and water to a boil. Add soaked garbanzo beans and soaking water, bring to a boil and simmer for 20 minutes or until tender. In another saucepan, place four cups of water and add lentils and onions and simmer for about 20 minutes. Add garbanzo bean and apricot mixture to lentils and simmer about 1½ hours or until garbanzo beans are tender. Add honey and salt, simmer 5 more minutes. Serve hot. Serves four.

BULGUR PILAV
Bulgur and vermicelli pilaf

½ cup butter
⅓ cup vermicelli
2 cups water

salt and pepper to taste
1 cup coarse bulgur

Sauté butter and vermicelli in saucepan until light brown. Add water and salt, bring to a boil. Add bulgur and simmer slowly until all the water is absorbed. Sprinkle top with black pepper and cover until ready to serve. Serve warm. Serves four.

ANOUSH ABOUR
Rice porridge with honey and nuts

¾ cup uncooked rice
1 cup honey
3½ cups water

¼ teaspoon cinnamon
½ cup almonds or walnuts, coarsely chopped

In a 3-quart saucepan add rice, honey, and water. Bring to a boil and simmer slowly uncovered about 1 hour or until rice is tender. Add cinnamon and spoon into four individual dessert bowls. Decorate tops with nuts. Serve warm or chilled. Serves four.

MEMIYE HALVA
Honey and cream of wheat dessert

½ cup butter
1 cup cream of wheat, uncooked
2 cups water

2 cups honey
cinnamon
walnuts, coarsely chopped

Stirring constantly, sauté butter and cream of wheat for about 5 minutes or until very light brown. Add water and honey, bring to a slow boil and simmer for about 15 minutes until all moisture is absorbed. Sprinkle generously with cinnamon and walnuts. Serve warm. Serves four.

French

One excellent feature of French cooking is that inexpensive foods are given the same loving treatment as the costly delicacies, and frequently taste even better. Rather than waste a shred of precious food, they'll dream up a masterpiece made from bits of this and that. The French look upon fresh vegetables not merely as necessary nutrients but as the gastronomical delights they are meant to be. What makes their cooking of green vegetables so different? When you prepare green vegetables the French way, you plunge them into a very large kettle full of rapidly boiling water. As soon as they are barely tender, you plunge them into cold water to stop the cooking and to set the fresh green color and texture. Just before serving you toss them briefly in hot butter and seasonings. Often vegetables are served with sauces. In these sauces all the flavors of the ingredients come together so smoothly that it's impossible at times to guess exactly what is there. Many of the sauces contain wine, and they believe the only reason to use wine in cooking is because of the natural savor it contributes. Therefore, any wine used for cooking should be a good one—not necessarily expensive—but full of natural flavor. A French meal can be very elegant, or may consist of hearty peasant fare from the provinces. Either way, the food will be finely prepared, for the French love to eat well.

FRENCH

TOMATE AVEC PIGNON
Tomatoes with pine nuts and parsley

4 large tomatoes
4 tablespoons olive oil
½ cup shelled pine nuts
5 tablespoons butter

1 cup parsley, minced
1 clove garlic, minced
salt and pepper

Halve the tomatoes, sprinkle them with salt and let them drain for 30 minutes. In a skillet, sauté in the olive oil the tomato halves for 2 to 3 minutes on each side, or until they are just softened. Transfer them cut sides up to an ovenproof serving dish and keep them hot in a preheated oven at 350 degrees. In the same skillet, sauté the pine nuts in the remaining olive oil for 2 minutes, or until they are lightly colored. Spoon all out into a small dish. Add butter to skillet and sauté with parsley, garlic and a dash of salt and pepper over moderate heat, stirring for about 5 minutes. Spoon the mixture on the tomatoes, top the tomatoes with the pine nuts, and serve immediately. Serves four.

OIGNONS À LA MONÉGASQUE
Chilled onions in raisin sauce

1½ pounds small white onions
4 tablespoons olive oil
1½ cups water
½ cup wine vinegar
3 tablespoons tomato paste
1 bay leaf

¼ teaspoon marjoram
2 tablespoons sugar
½ cup seedless raisins
1½ teaspoons salt
½ teaspoon freshly ground black pepper

Pick onions of uniform size, and peel. Heat the oil in a saucepan; add onions and toss until coated. Add the water, vinegar, tomato paste, bay leaf, marjoram, sugar, raisins, salt and pepper, and bring to a boil. Cook with cover over low heat, shaking pan frequently for 30 minutes. Chill before serving. Serves four.

POTAGE CREME NIVERNAISE
Cream of carrot soup

2 cups carrots, thinly sliced
4 tablespoons butter
1 teaspoon sugar
1 teaspoon salt
½ cup water

2 tablespoons flour
dash of pepper
2¼ cups milk
½ cup cream

Combine in saucepan: carrots, 2 tablespoons butter, sugar, salt and water. Cover and simmer until tender about 15 to 20 minutes. While carrots are cooking melt in another saucepan 2 tablespoons butter; blend in flour and dash of pepper. Stir over medium heat until smooth and bubbly. Remove from heat and stir in milk. Bring to boil and boil 1 minute, stirring constantly. Combine contents of both saucepans and put through an electric blender or very fine sieve. Blend in cream; heat and serve. Serves four.

27

SOUFFLE AUX EPINARDS
Spinach souffle

1 cup cooked spinach, finely chopped
4 tablespoons butter
2 teaspoons salt
dash of nutmeg
3 tablespoons flour
1¼ cups milk

dash of cayenne
dash of Worcestershire sauce
5 eggs, separated
3 tablespoons Swiss cheese, finely shredded

Season spinach with 1 tablespoon of the butter, 1 teaspoon of salt, and dash of nutmeg. Cook over heat to remove any excess moisture. Melt 3 remaining tablespoons of butter in a small pan. Blend in flour and cook until it bubbles and is lightly browned. Gradually stir in milk, 1 teaspoon salt, and seasonings. Cook over low heat, stirring constantly, for 10 minutes, or until thickened. Gradually beat in the well-beaten egg yolks, a little at a time, until well blended. Add spinach mixture and cool. Fold in egg whites—beaten until stiff but not dry. Pour into a greased 2-quart souffle dish. Sprinkle the top with grated cheese and bake in a moderate oven at 375 degrees for 40 minutes, or until the top is browned and the souffle is nicely puffed. Serve immediately. Serves four.

SOUPE AU CRESSON
Watercress soup

4 potatoes
1 quart water
2 cups scalded milk
salt
1 bunch watercress

4 tablespoons butter
4 tablespoons fresh chervil or parsley, chopped
dash of ground pepper

Peel the potatoes and cut them into small pieces. Boil in a quart of water. Do not strain but mash them in the water in the saucepan. Add the milk and season with salt. Trim the stem from the watercress and wash well. Add the leaves to the soup and cook for 10 minutes. Just before serving, add the butter, chopped chervil and a dash of freshly ground pepper. Serves four.

FLAMICHE AUX POIREAUX
Leek pie

10 leeks, white part thinly sliced
2½ tablespoons butter
salt and pepper to taste
1 tablespoon flour

1½ cups light cream
2 tablespoons mushrooms, diced
1 9-inch unbaked pie shell (see page 39)

Sauté leeks in 1 tablespoon butter until almost soft. Season with salt and pepper. Melt 1 tablespoon butter, blend in flour and slowly add cream, stirring to the boiling point. Cook 5 minutes or until thickened, stirring constantly. Mix leeks with white sauce, add mushrooms and simmer 4 minutes. Pour into pie shell, dot with remaining ½ tablespoon of butter and bake in a 400-degree oven 30 minutes or until crust is golden on the edges. Serve at once. Serves four.

HARICOTS VERTS À LA NIÇOISE
Green beans in tomato sauce

¼ cup olive oil
1 clove garlic, finely minced
1 cup onions, chopped
¼ cup green peppers, diced
2 cups canned strained tomatoes
1 bay leaf

2 tablespoons parsley, minced
¼ teaspoon sugar
2 teaspoons salt
¼ teaspoon freshly ground black pepper
1½ pounds green beans, cut in 2-inch
   lengths

Heat the oil in a saucepan; add the garlic, onions, green peppers and sauté 5 minutes. Add the tomatoes, bay leaf, parsley, sugar, salt and pepper. Bring to a boil; then cook over low heat 15 minutes. Add the string beans, cover and cook over low heat 45 minutes. Season to taste. Serves four.

Greek

Vegetarianism was introduced among the Greeks by the philosopher Pythagoras. During a visit to India in the sixth century B.C., he was inspired in both his philosophy and his eating habits by Buddhism. Since Greece is chiefly agricultural, the country people can live almost exclusively from the soil if need be, enjoying a highly nutritious diet of olives, bread, fruit and nuts. In Greece, the largest and most elaborate meal is served at midday, when the cities close for a three- to four-hour break. This meal usually consists of soup, salad, a main entrée, with side dishes of vegetables and freshly baked bread. For dessert, the fresh fruits of the season are served. The Greeks excel in appetizers and have a wonderful array of nibble foods, known as *mezedakia*. These are set out in tavernas, where the people gather at the end of the day for a refreshing drink and to enjoy the company and conversation of their friends. An interesting Greek custom, observed on the first day of the New Year, is the serving of *vasilopitta*. This is a cake with a single gold piece inserted in the dough before baking. According to tradition, the cake must be cut in equal pieces, one for each family member, and then eaten. Whoever finds the gold coin in his piece becomes the lucky one in the household for the year.

GREEK

DOMATES YEMISTES
Tomatoes stuffed with rice

8 large firm tomatoes
½ cup olive oil
2 medium onions, chopped
1 cup rice
1½ teaspoons salt

freshly ground black pepper
½ cup water
⅓ cup pine nuts
2 tablespoons fresh dill, chopped
2 tablespoons fresh parsley, minced

Carefully slice tops from tomatoes, saving tops to use as caps when the tomatoes are stuffed. Scoop out the pulp and save, leaving enough for a thick shell. Brush the tomatoes with olive oil and sprinkle with salt. Place in baking pan or large shallow casserole. Simmer the onions in olive oil in a heavy saucepan until soft. Add the rice, salt, pepper, water and the scooped out pulp from the tomatoes. Cover saucepan and bring to a boil, reduce heat and cook 10 minutes. Add remaining ingredients. Spoon this mixture—it should be mushy—into the hollowed tomatoes. Replace tomato tops and brush with a little oil. Bake uncovered at 350 degrees for 1 hour. Serves four.

SPANSKORIZO
Spinach with rice

1 cup uncooked rice
2 cups boiling water
2 teaspoons salt
2 bunches spinach, washed and cooked
2 leeks or 4 green onions

1 small onion, chopped
¼ cup olive oil
1 teaspoon dill or parsley, minced
2 tablespoons pine nuts
1 tablespoon butter

Cook rice in boiling water with 1 teaspoon salt for 15 minutes. Set aside. Cook spinach in the usual way, drain and chop. Slice leeks or green onions including part of green section. Cook leeks and chopped onion in olive oil until soft; season with 1 teaspoon salt. Combine this with cooked spinach, dill and pine nuts. Stir spinach and leek mixture into rice and add butter. Cover pan with clean cloth towel and place over very low heat for 10 minutes. Serve with sliced tomatoes and artichokes with an oil and lemon juice dressing. Serves four.

LAHANIKA YAHNI
Vegetable stew

5 onions, chopped
2 cloves garlic, finely minced
⅓ cup olive oil
6 potatoes, peeled and sliced
4 tomatoes, chopped

1 cup tomato sauce
½ pound green beans, cut
salt and pepper to taste
2 tablespoons parsley, minced
½ teaspoon crushed red pepper

Cook onions and garlic in oil until soft. Add remaining ingredients; cook covered over low heat until potatoes are soft. Add small amount of water during cooking as needed. Note: Other vegetables that may be added to this stew in place of, or in addition to, beans are squash, eggplant, okra, green pepper or cabbage. Serves four.

SALATA
Cauliflower salad

1 medium cauliflower
4 small onions
¼ cup olive oil
2 cups pared, sliced carrots
1 clove garlic, minced
1 cup dry white wine
1 cup water

¼ cup lemon juice
½ cup tomato paste
1 bay leaf
¼ teaspoon coriander seed
1½ teaspoons salt
¼ teaspoon pepper

Separate cauliflower into flowerets and wash well. Drain. Slice onions and separate into rings. Heat oil in enameled or stainless steel saucepan over low heat. Add onions, carrots and garlic. Cook 5 minutes, stirring occasionally. Add wine, water, lemon juice, tomato paste, bay leaf, coriander seed, salt and pepper. Bring to a boil. Add cauliflower. Simmer 10 to 15 minutes or until cauliflower is just tender. Transfer cauliflower to serving dish with slotted spoon. Heat liquid until the volume is reduced to about 1½ cups. Remove bay leaf. Correct seasoning of liquid to taste. Pour over cauliflower in serving dish. Chill several hours. When ready to serve, garnish with parsley. Serves four.

LAHANA YAHNI
Braised cabbage with tomatoes

½ head Savoy or green cabbage
2 medium onions, chopped
¼ cup olive oil
2 cups strained canned tomatoes

2 tablespoons parsley, minced
2 large carrots, peeled and diced
salt and pepper to taste

Cut cabbage in quarters, wash and drain. Cook onions in olive oil until golden. Add remaining ingredients, cover and cook 20 to 30 minutes until all vegetables are tender. Serves four.

BAMIES ME DOMATES
Okra with tomatoes

1 medium onion, sliced
¼ cup olive oil
1 pound okra, washed and trimmed
4 medium tomatoes, chopped
1 cup tomato juice

¼ teaspoon thyme
1 teaspoon salt
dash of black pepper
1 teaspoon lemon juice

Sauté onion in oil until soft. Add remaining ingredients and simmer slowly for one hour. Serves four.

KOLOKITHAKIA YAHNI
Zucchini with tomatoes

1½ pounds zucchini squash
2 onions, sliced
6 tablespoons olive oil
4 large tomatoes, chopped

2 tablespoons parsley, minced
1 teaspoon salt
dash of coarse red pepper

Wash squash thoroughly and cut into 2-inch pieces. Cook onions in oil until golden but not browned. Add squash, tomatoes, parsley, salt and pepper. Simmer uncovered about 30 minutes. Can be eaten hot or cold. Serves four.

PATATES ME DOMATES
Potatoes with tomatoes

4 potatoes, peeled and sliced
2 onions, sliced
3 tablespoons olive oil

2 tablespoons parsley, minced
1 teaspoon salt
3 medium tomatoes, peeled and diced

Place potatoes and onions with olive oil in a heavy skillet. Cook slowly until golden and tender but not browned. Add parsley, salt, tomatoes and cook covered over low heat until potatoes are very tender and sauce is thickened. Serves four.

MELITZANES YEMISTES
Eggplant stuffed with tomatoes

2 small eggplants, each 6 or 7 inches
   long
½ cup olive oil
2 large tomatoes, peeled and chopped
2 cloves garlic, crushed
½ cup onion, chopped

1 teaspoon parsley, minced
½ teaspoon dried mint
¾ teaspoon salt
pepper to taste
½ cup fine bread crumbs

Cut the eggplants in half lengthwise, carefully cutting away stems. Scoop out pulp and save, leaving a thick shell. Sauté the eggplant shells in olive oil just until outside is softened. Remove carefully, place with hollowed side up in a shallow casserole or baking pan. To same oil add tomatoes, garlic, onions, parsley, mint, the diced eggplant pulp and salt and pepper to taste. Cook until mixture is soft and fill eggplant shells. Sprinkle crumbs over top. Bake at 350 degrees about 45 minutes or until eggplants are very soft. Serves four.

MELITZANESALATA
Eggplant caviar

1 large eggplant
1 small onion, finely minced
2 cloves garlic, crushed
2 tablespoons olive oil

1 teaspoon lemon juice
salt to taste
1 tablespoon parsley, finely minced
½ cup yogurt or sour cream

Toast whole eggplant over medium flame of a gas burner, or bake in oven for 45 minutes at 350 degrees, turning occasionally until the outer skin is wrinkled and the eggplant is noticeably soft. Peel and drain eggplant. Blend with spoon eggplant with onion, garlic, oil, lemon juice, salt and parsley. Add yogurt or sour cream and blend thoroughly. Serve as an hors d'oeuvre with chips or Middle Eastern cracker bread. Makes about 2 cups.

PIPERIES SKARA
Green pepper relish

4 large green peppers, cut in squares
1 medium onion, sliced
2 cloves garlic
¼ cup olive oil

salt and pepper to taste
2 tablespoons vinegar
dash of oregano

Sauté peppers, sliced onions and garlic cloves in olive oil. Simmer over lowered heat until onion is soft. Remove and discard garlic. Turn off heat. Sprinkle with salt, pepper, vinegar and oregano. Serve cold as a relish or vegetable.

PLAKI
Beans in tomato sauce

1 pound dried navy beans
½ cup olive oil
3 cloves garlic
4 medium onions, thickly sliced
¼ teaspoon marjoram or oregano

¼ teaspoon thyme
1 bay leaf, crumbled
2 tablespoons parsley, minced
6 tomatoes, peeled and diced
1 teaspoon salt, or more to taste

Soak beans overnight in water enough to cover. Drain thoroughly, wash with cold water, and set aside. Heat olive oil in a heavy iron pot or Dutch oven. Add minced garlic, onions, and the herbs. Sauté until onions are soft but not brown. Add tomatoes and simmer until well blended. Add drained beans and water enough to cover beans. Bring to a boil, turn the heat as low as possible and simmer covered for 1 hour. Add more water if needed. Remove cover, add salt and simmer 1 hour longer. Serves four.

TZATZIKI
Cucumber and yogurt cold soup

2 cucumbers
4 cups yogurt
2 garlic cloves, crushed
2 tablespoons olive oil

1 tablespoon vinegar
½ teaspoon salt
1 tablespoon dill, minced

Peel and coarsely grate cucumbers. Add remaining ingredients and blend thoroughly. Chill in refrigerator until serving. Serves four.

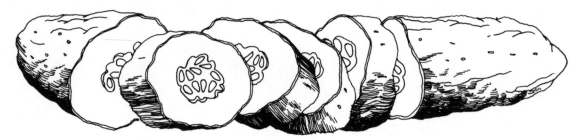

YIAOURTOPETA
Yogurt cake

½ cup butter
1 cup sugar
2½ cups self-rising cake flour
1 cup yogurt

4 eggs
grated rind of ½ lemon
confectioners' sugar

Place butter and sugar in bowl, beat until creamy smooth. Slowly add self-rising cake flour and yogurt, beating to blend. Add eggs one at a time, beating until smooth. Add lemon rind and blend. Pour into greased and floured 9 × 13 × 2-inch pan, and place in preheated oven at 350 degrees. Bake 50 minutes or until toothpick inserted in the center comes out clean. Let cake stand in pan 10 minutes, then turn out on a rack. Dust with confectioners' sugar.

MELOPETA
Honey pie

Pastry:

1½ cups sifted flour

¼ teaspoon salt

½ cup butter

1 egg, well beaten

Blend flour with salt and cut in butter until it becomes the size of peas. Add the well-beaten egg and knead with fingers until well blended. Chill. Roll out between sheets of waxed paper. Place in a 9-inch pie pan, making the pastry stand up around the edge. Chill again for 30 minutes. Place pie shell in hot oven, at 450 degrees for 10 minutes. Remove pie shell from oven and lower temperature to 325 degrees.

Filling:

1½ pounds ricotta cheese

½ cup honey

¼ teaspoon cinnamon

5 eggs

Combine cheese, honey, cinnamon and beat until well blended. Beat in eggs, one at a time. Pour mixture in pie shell and bake 50 minutes or until a knife inserted in the center comes out clean. Serve cold.

TYROPETA
Cream cheese and yogurt pie

½ pound cream cheese

1 cup plain yogurt

1 teaspoon vanilla

3 tablespoons honey

1 9-inch baked pie shell (see page 39)

Have cream cheese at room temperature. In a bowl, cream the cheese very well. Add yogurt a little at a time, mixing until smooth. Stir in honey and vanilla. Pour into baked pie shell and refrigerate for 24 hours.

Indian

Since food and religion in India are closely interwoven, the cuisine takes on certain metaphysical overtones. The people have a strong awareness that their nourishment comes from God, and the sharing of food is thus a religious or spiritual act. On occasions such as weddings, funerals and betrothals, the family is expected to provide food not only for the guests, but also for innumerable beggars that gather outside the event. Differences between Northern and Southern India exist not only in culture, language and climate, but in the style of cooking as well. In the cooler Northern regions of India, food preparation is more elaborate than in the warm Southern regions where people live mainly on vegetables. The Northern dishes taste richer and hotter, with rice used as an important staple, and with large amounts of coconut oil and coconut milk added in cooking. Since refrigeration was limited in India, the people discovered that foods prepared with certain spices would not spoil so easily. One such ingredient, curry, possesses a piquant hotness that stimulates perspiration, one of nature's ways to cool the body. Many people believe curry powder to be a particular spice or herb that has been ground up. In reality, it is made from a combination of spices, herbs and aromatic seeds which usually include cumin, coriander, cloves, cardamom, turmeric, ginger, cayenne and garlic. An Indian curry means any dish, with a richly spiced sauce, that is carefully cooked to blend the spices and ingredients into a delicious and satisfying meal.

INDIAN

ANDA KARI
Mushroom and egg curry

½ pound small mushrooms
6 eggs, hard-boiled
1 large onion, chopped
4 tablespoons butter
2 tablespoons chopped parsley
1 teaspoon turmeric

2 teaspoons curry powder
1 teaspoon ginger
3 large tomatoes, sliced
1 cup yogurt
2 tablespoons lemon juice
salt to taste

Soak mushrooms in lightly salted water for about 15 minutes. Hard-boil the eggs and halve lengthwise. Set aside. In a saucepan, sauté the onions in butter until lightly golden. Add parsley, turmeric, curry powder and ginger and allow to cook for a few minutes. Add the tomatoes and the yogurt. Cook for about 10 minutes and add the drained mushrooms. Cover and cook another 15 minutes. Add egg halves to saucepan. Cook for another 15 minutes. Just before removing from heat, add lemon juice and salt to taste. Serves four.

DHAL CHANNA
Split peas, with curry and mint

1 cup yellow split peas
3 cups water
1 teaspoon turmeric
1½ teaspoons salt
½ teaspoon crushed red pepper
　(optional)

1 tablespoon butter
1 large onion, chopped
1 teaspoon ground ginger
1 teaspoon curry powder
2 tablespoons fresh mint, chopped

Soak the split peas in water for 30 minutes. Boil the 3 cups of water then add the drained split peas. Add the turmeric, salt and crushed red pepper. Lower heat and allow to simmer until the split peas are soft, about one hour. Heat the butter in a frying pan and add the onions, ginger, curry powder and mint. Sauté this mixture for about 5 minutes. Add to the split peas and serve hot. Serves four.

ALU TAMATAR
Potato and tomato curry

1½ tablespoons butter
5 slices fresh ginger root
2 medium onions, sliced
1 teaspoon turmeric
2 teaspoons curry powder

2½ teaspoons salt
2 tablespoons parsley, chopped
1½ pounds small white potatoes
5 tomatoes, sliced
1 cup hot water

Heat the butter in a saucepan; add the sliced ginger and onions. Sauté until onions are a light golden color. Add turmeric, curry powder, salt and parsley. Cook for 5 minutes on low heat. Add potatoes and tomatoes; continue cooking for another 10 minutes. Add the hot water and cook until the potatoes are tender. Serves four.

VINDALOO
Curry paste spread

8 tablespoons ground coriander
2 tablespoons turmeric
2 tablespoons black pepper
4 teaspoons ground ginger
3 tablespoons salt
4 tablespoons chick-pea flour
4 teaspoons ground cumin

½ teaspoon cayenne pepper
3 tablespoons mustard powder
1 tablespoon garlic powder
4 tablespoons sugar
white vinegar as needed
1 cup oil

Blend all the ingredients except oil together with enough vinegar to make a thick paste. Heat the oil in a large skillet. Cook the paste in oil over moderate heat, stirring continuously until it becomes thick and dryer. This will take about 15 to 20 minutes. Cool and bottle tightly to use as needed. This makes a very different and delicious spread for crackers or toast. It can also be used in place of curry powder in many recipes.

DHAL KARI
Lentil and egg curry

1 cup dried lentils
3 tablespoons butter
2 onions, sliced
1 tablespoon curry powder

¾ cup water
1 teaspoon salt
6 hard-boiled eggs, sliced

Soak the lentils overnight in water enough to cover. Drain well. Melt the butter in a saucepan; add the onions and curry powder and sauté for 10 minutes stirring frequently. Add ¾ cup water and lentils. Cover and cook over low heat for 45 minutes, or until the lentils are tender. Add the salt and sliced eggs and gently mix. Cook over low heat for another 5 minutes. Serves four.

PULAO
Feast day rice

1 cup butter
3 cups boiling water
¼ teaspoon saffron
1 medium onion, chopped
1 inch cinnamon stick
2 whole cloves
½ teaspoon ground ginger

1 tablespoon ground cumin
½ teaspoon garlic powder
5 shelled cardamom seeds
2 cups long grain rice
½ cup plain yogurt
1 teaspoon salt

Heat shortening in a large heavy pot with a tightly fitting cover. While the butter is heating, bring water to a boil. When the water is hot, dip ½ cup and soak the saffron in it. Set aside for later use. Add onions to hot butter; sauté until golden. Add cinnamon, cloves, ginger, cumin, garlic and cardamom. Stir continuously for 3 to 4 minutes. Add raw rice, stirring continuously for about 10 minutes but be careful not to burn the rice at this stage. Next add yogurt, then the saffron water, and the remainder of the boiling water and the salt. Cover with a damp cloth that is folded into four or eight layers, lower heat to simmer, cover cloth with the pot cover and cook for approximately 20 minutes, or until all water is absorbed and the rice is tender. Serves four.

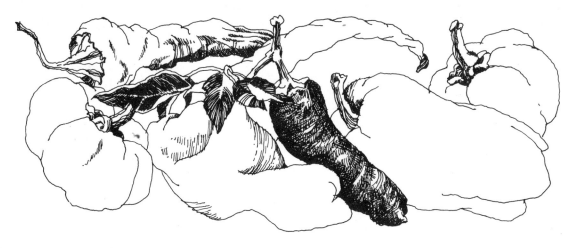

THUCAHLEY FOOGATHS
Stewed tomatoes

4 tablespoons butter
1 onion, chopped
2 cloves garlic, minced
¼ teaspoon powdered ginger
¼ teaspoon ground chili pepper

4 tomatoes, peeled and chopped
1 teaspoon salt
1 tablespoon fresh or dried grated
 coconut

Melt the butter in a skillet. Add the onion, garlic, ginger and chili peppers. Sauté for 5 minutes, stirring occasionally. Add the tomatoes, salt and coconut. Cook over low heat for 15 minutes, or until the liquid is absorbed. Serve as a vegetable side dish. Serves four.

BAINGAN KARI
Eggplant and yogurt curry

1 large eggplant
2 medium onions, sliced
4 tablespoons butter
2 cups yogurt
1 tablespoon tomato paste
2 cloves garlic, minced

½ teaspoon ground ginger
½ teaspoon ground cloves
½ teaspoon ground cumin
1 cup water
salt to taste

Cut eggplant in 2-inch squares. In a saucepan, sauté the sliced onion in butter until golden. Add remaining ingredients, mixing thoroughly. Cook for about 20 minutes. Serves four.

VADAY
Lentil appetizer

1 cup lentils or split peas
2 small onions, finely chopped
2 fresh green chilies

½ teaspoon ginger
oil for deep frying

Soak the lentils in water overnight. Drain them and grind well in a blender or mortar. Let the ground lentils stand for about an hour. Mix in the onions, chilies, ginger and salt to taste. Form the mixture into 1-inch balls and flatten on an oiled surface to prevent sticking. Deep fry until crisp in hot oil. Drain on paper towel and serve hot. These may be made earlier in the day and reheated in a hot oven just before serving. Excellent with a glass of wine. Serves four.

TIKKI CHANA DHAL
Chick-pea cutlets

1 cup dried chick-peas
4 cups water
1 large onion, minced
2 green chilies, seeded and chopped
1½ tablespoons coriander leaves,
  chopped
¼ teaspoon turmeric
¼ teaspoon cayenne pepper

1½ teaspoons ground cumin
pinch of sugar
salt to taste
3 eggs
1 cup flour
breadcrumbs
½ cup vegetable oil

Wash chick-peas, cover with 4 cups water and soak overnight. Bring to a boil the water in which the chick-peas soaked and cook slowly until tender, about 1 hour. Drain thoroughly and grind in a food mill to make a thick paste. To this mixture add onion, chilies, coriander, turmeric, cayenne pepper, cumin, sugar, salt and one egg; mix thoroughly. Chill 1 hour in refrigerator. Form mixture into ½-inch thick heart-shaped cutlets about 2 inches in diameter. In a small bowl, beat 2 eggs well. Roll cutlets in flour, dip them in the beaten eggs, and roll them in bread crumbs. Heat oil in a large skillet and fry cutlets gently over moderate heat until golden brown, turning once. Remove cutlets and drain on paper towels. Serve hot with tomato and cucumber slices and lemon juice. Makes 16 small cutlets, serving four.

Israeli

When the state of Israel was created in 1948, people of more than 80 nationalities gathered to become its new citizens. Naturally they wanted to eat as they had in the past, and so they brought along traditional recipes from their former Jewish communities. Since most Israeli homes and restaurants devoutly observe the Jewish *kashrut*, dietary laws prohibiting both meat and dairy products at the same meal, two separate sets of dishes must be kept by housewives and chefs. There is even a village in Israel inhabited entirely by vegetarians. These dietary laws have inspired Jewish cooks to develop intriguing vegetable dishes for the dairy meals. The *falafel*—a chick-pea patty served in *peta*, a pocket-type bread, and often called the "Israeli hot dog"—is one such favorite of Middle Eastern vegetarians. Israel has taken amazing agricultural strides by developing truck gardens, fruit orchards and groves of banana, avocado, and orange trees. Much of this success is inspired by the kibbutz, a unique experiment of communal endeavor, where each member works for all the others as well as for himself.

ISRAELI

PETA
Pocket bread

1 package active dry yeast
1¼ cups warm water
½ teaspoon salt

3½ cups flour
¼ cup poppy or caraway seeds

In a bowl blend yeast and water; let stand 5 minutes. Stir in salt and gradually mix in enough flour to form a stiff dough. Turn dough out onto a floured board and knead until smooth, about 5 minutes; add more flour as needed to prevent sticking. Cut into 8 equal pieces. Keep dough lightly covered with a cloth. On a lightly floured board, shape each piece of dough into a smooth ball. Flatten each slightly; then with a floured rolling pin, roll each into a circle about 5 inches in diameter. Dampen top and sprinkle with seeds if desired. Place rounds about 1 inch apart on greased sheets. Cover rounds very lightly with a cloth. Let rise in a warm place until puffy looking, about 45 minutes. Lift cloth once or twice during rising time to make sure it isn't sticking to the dough. Bake in a 450-degree oven for 8 to 10 minutes or until lightly browned. Stack in a pile when baked. Makes 8 rounds.

LATKES
Potato pancakes

2 cups grated raw potatoes, measure
   after draining
2 eggs, beaten
1 teaspoon salt
1 heaping tablespoon flour or matzo
   meal

pinch of baking powder
1 small onion, grated
butter

Combine all ingredients. Mix well. Drop pancake mixture by the tablespoonful onto a hot skillet generously greased with butter or shortening. If you like thin, crisp pancakes, flatten with the back of a spoon. Fry on both sides until brown. Serve piping hot with sour cream or with applesauce. Serves four.

FRUCHT TZIMMES
Dried fruit and rice dessert

1½ pounds mixed dried fruit such as
   prunes, peaches, pears, apricots and
   raisins
½ cup brown rice
4 tablespoons honey
¼ teaspoon cinnamon

½ teaspoon salt
2 cups boiling water
2 tablespoons flour
2 tablespoons butter
1 cup water

Wash fruit in hot water and drain. Combine with rice, honey, cinnamon, salt and the 2 cups boiling water. Bring to the boiling point, then reduce heat and simmer slowly until the rice is tender, about 20 to 30 minutes. It may be necessary to add a little water. Heat flour in a small skillet until light brown, stirring constantly to prevent burning. Stir in butter, then slowly add 1 cup water, stirring constantly. When mixture is smooth and thick, add to the fruit. Cook until the fruit liquid has thickened. Remove to a casserole and brown lightly under the broiler flame for a few minutes. Serve hot. Serves four.

SÜSSE FASOLYES
Sweet limas with honey

1½ cups dried lima beans
1 teaspoon salt

½ cup honey

Cover beans with cold water and soak overnight. Drain, cover with cold water and add salt. Bring to a boil in a covered saucepan. Reduce heat and simmer for 1 hour. Add honey. Cook uncovered until beans are tender and golden brown, about 1 hour. Serves four.

CHAROSIS
Apple and walnut appetizer

2 tart apples
½ cup walnuts
¼ teaspoon cinnamon

1 teaspoon honey
1 tablespoon sweet Concord wine
matzo wafers

Pare and core apples. Chop apples and nuts together finely. Add cinnamon, honey and wine. This makes about 2 cups. It is served at the Passover seder as a symbol of the mortar and bricks that the Hebrews were forced to make for the pyramids and cities of Egypt. Serve 1 teaspoon per person on matzos.

LABNA LATKES
Cheese pancakes

½ pound dry cottage cheese
6 eggs, separated
4 tablespoons matzo meal

½ teaspoon salt
butter

Rub cottage cheese through a sieve. Stir egg yolks into the cheese. Add matzo meal and salt. Mix well. Beat egg whites until stiff and fold into the cheese mixture. Drop from a tablespoon onto a hot buttered skillet. Fry on both sides until lightly browned. Serve hot with syrup, honey or cinnamon-sugar mix. Serves four.

FALAFEL
Chick-pea patties

Patties:

1 pound dried chick-peas
3 slices bread
2 hot peppers
3 sprigs parsley

3 eggs, beaten
garlic powder, salt and pepper to taste
peanut oil for frying
pocket bread (see page 50)

Soak peas for 12 hours in cold water. Remove skins and grind peas with bread, peppers and parsley. Add eggs and seasonings. Let stand 1 hour. Make into balls about the size of a silver dollar, round but flat enough to fry. Fry in peanut oil and serve hot in pocket bread with falafel sauce, garnished with chopped parsley. Serves four.

Falafel sauce:

1 cup tomato sauce
1 hot pepper, finely chopped
salt to taste

Mix all ingredients and simmer 10 minutes.

Italian

There is much debate as to which country deserves credit for inventing pastas, but undeniably the Italians have made them famous. With pastas, there are those you can buy and those you can make. A good Italian cook would never hesitate to do both. Pasta in some form is a regular part of the daily Italian menu and can be served in a great variety of interesting and tempting ways. The cuisine varies from a gentle rich cooking in the North, which often uses rice and polenta, to the spicier food of the South where tomatoes have a greater popularity. Olive oil and herbs, however, are used in practically every Italian recipe. Their food is perfumed with oregano, rosemary, basil and fennel, which give Italian cooking its distinctive aromatic quality. Their olive oil comes from the green species of this tree from which the oil is extracted by pressing the fruit. The black olive is used only for eating. It is either dried in the sun and cured with salt and olive oil, or it is preserved in brine. The olive tree must be ten years old before it can bear fruit, and from then on it continues to produce for generations. Anything that springs from the earth has a special charm for the Italians: fruits, vegetables, herbs and flowers. They have a strong seasonal respect for the good things of the earth. The first oranges, the first thin stalks of asparagus, the early red ripe cherries—Italians taste the months go by in time with nature.

ITALIAN

CAPONATA
Eggplant with tomatoes

1 eggplant, cut in ½-inch cubes
salt
¼ cup olive oil
1 cup celery, diced
⅓ cup onion, diced
3 tablespoons Burgundy wine
juice of ½ lemon

1 tablespoon sugar
2 tablespoons tomato paste
1½ cups Italian style tomatoes
6 stuffed green olives, chopped
freshly ground pepper
dash of crushed ground red pepper

Sprinkle eggplant cubes with salt and let drain in colander 30 minutes, then pat dry with a towel. Heat 2 tablespoons oil in heavy skillet, add celery and cook 10 minutes. Add onion and cook 10 minutes longer. Remove vegetables and set aside. Add remaining 2 tablespoons oil to skillet, heat, add eggplant and sauté 10 minutes. Return vegetables to skillet. Stir in wine, lemon juice, sugar, tomato paste, tomatoes, olives, and salt and pepper to taste. Bring to a boil, reduce heat and simmer uncovered about 20 minutes or until thickened. Stir occasionally to prevent sticking. Serve immediately or turn into a glass dish and chill well before serving cold. Serves four.

PIZZA
Yeast dough, with tomato sauce and cheese

Dough:
1 pkg. active dry yeast

1 cup lukewarm water

2 teaspoons sugar

3½ cups flour

1 tablespoon oil

1½ teaspoons salt

Dissolve yeast in water and add sugar. Then add 1½ cups of the flour. Beat until blended. Mix in shortening and salt; add remaining 2 cups of flour. Mix thoroughly. Knead on floured board until smooth, about 10 minutes. Place dough in a greased bowl; turn once to bring greased side up. Cover with a damp cloth and let rise until more than double in bulk, about 2 hours. Knead down and place in refrigerator about 30 minutes. Divide dough in half and form into balls. Roll each on a lightly floured board to form 12-inch circles. Transfer rolled dough to two greased pizza pans.

Sauce:
1½ cups Italian style tomatoes

2 cloves garlic, finely minced

¼ teaspoon sweet basil

½ teaspoon oregano

½ teaspoon salt

¼ teaspoon pepper

Drain juice from tomatoes and save. Mash the tomatoes with a fork. Add garlic, sweet basil, oregano, salt and pepper. Stir in 8 tablespoons of the tomato juice. Spread sauce on each circle of dough.

Cheese topping:
1 pound mozzarella cheese, grated

2 tablespoons olive oil

2 tablespoons grated Parmesan cheese

½ teaspoon oregano

Arrange half of the mozzarella cheese on top of the two circles. Sprinkle 1 tablespoon olive oil, 1 tablespoon Parmesan cheese and ¼ teaspoon oregano over each circle. Place in a preheated 425-degree oven and bake for 20 to 25 minutes. Cut in wedges and serve immediately. Makes two 12-inch pizzas.

RAVIOLI
Cheese-filled pasta

Tomato sauce:

2 onions, sliced
1 clove garlic
4 tablespoons olive oil
1 sprig sweet basil

3½ cups canned strained tomatoes
½ teaspoon sugar
salt and pepper to taste

Fry onion and garlic in oil about 5 minutes; add basil. Strain tomatoes through sieve; add and simmer for 45 minutes or until tomatoes are cooked to a thick sauce. Stir frequently. Add sugar, salt and pepper; stir thoroughly. Simmer 15 minutes.

Filling:

1¼ cups ricotta cheese
¼ cup Parmesan cheese, grated
2 eggs beaten

½ cup cooked beets, grated
1 tablespoon raisins, chopped
½ teaspoon salt

Combine all filling ingredients and mix thoroughly.

Pasta:

1 cup flour
2 eggs

Mix flour and eggs together to form paste for the dough. After kneading this thoroughly, roll it out thin and cut into 2-inch squares. Spread filling mixture over half of each section of dough. Moisten edges and fold the other half over the filling, pressing the edges together firmly. Cook in rapidly boiling water, about 10 minutes or until dough is tender. Remove carefully with perforated spoon; place serving portions on individual heated plates. Top with hot tomato sauce and sprinkle with grated Parmesan cheese. Serve very hot. Makes twelve ravioli and serves four.

LINGUINI ZUCCHINI
Noodles with zucchini and tomatoes

1 onion, chopped
1 clove garlic, minced
3 tablespoons olive oil
1 cup sliced pimentos, drained
3 tablespoons minced parsley
¼ teaspoon fennel seed, crushed
½ teaspoon marjoram leaves

2 cups canned pear-shaped tomatoes
1½ teaspoons sugar
¼ cup dry red wine
¼ teaspoon each salt and pepper
4 medium-sized zucchini, thinly sliced
8 ounces spinach noodles
freshly grated Parmesan cheese

In a frying pan, cook the onion and garlic in the olive oil until onion is limp. Add the pimentos, parsley, fennel seed, marjoram, tomatoes, sugar, wine, salt and pepper. Bring to boiling, stirring to break up tomatoes. Then reduce heat, cover, and simmer for 30 minutes. Stir in the zucchini and cook covered, until tender, about 5 to 7 minutes. Cook the noodles in boiling salted water according to package directions. Drain well, then place noodles in a serving bowl. Spoon sauce over noodles. Mix gently, then serve. Accompany with freshly grated Parmesan cheese to sprinkle generously over servings. Serves four.

GNOCCHI ALLA GRANERESE
Noodles with walnuts

1 cup ground walnuts
1 clove garlic, minced
1 pound ricotta cheese
1 cup grated Parmesan cheese

2 teaspoons salt
½ teaspoon black pepper
1 pound broad noodles

Roll or pound the walnuts and garlic on a board or in a mortar until a paste is formed. Place in a large bowl. Add both cheeses, salt and pepper. Mix well. Boil the noodles in salted water until tender, about 10 minutes. Drain. Add to the walnut mixture and toss lightly with two forks until the noodles are well coated. Place on a heated platter and serve. Serves four.

MELENZANA LASAGNE
Vegetable lasagne

1 large onion, chopped
2 cloves garlic, minced
1 medium eggplant, diced
¼ pound mushrooms, sliced
5 tablespoons olive oil
2 cups canned, strained pear-shaped
   tomatoes
1 cup tomato sauce
½ cup dry red wine
1 medium carrot, shredded
¼ cup parsley, minced

2 teaspoons oregano leaves
1 teaspoon basil leaves
1 teaspoon salt
¼ teaspoon pepper
9 wide, cooked lasagne noodles
2 cups ricotta cheese
8 ounces mozzarella cheese, cut in thin
   slices
1½ cups grated Parmesan cheese

In a large frying pan, cook the onion, garlic, eggplant, and mushrooms in the olive oil over medium heat for 15 minutes; stir frequently. Stir in the tomatoes, tomato sauce, wine, carrot, parsley, oregano, basil, salt and pepper. Bring to boiling, stirring to break up tomatoes; then reduce heat and simmer, covered, for 30 minutes. Increase heat and boil to reduce sauce until it measures 5 cups; set aside. Butter a 9 × 13-inch baking dish. Spread about a fourth of the sauce over the bottom. Arrange an even layer of 3 noodles on top. Dot noodles with a third of the ricotta. Arrange an even layer of one-third of the mozzarella and sprinkle with one-fourth of the Parmesan. Repeat procedure twice. Spread remaining sauce evenly over top and sprinkle with remaining Parmesan. Bake lasagne uncovered in a 350-degree oven for 45 minutes or until bubbly. Let stand 5 minutes, then cut into squares to serve. Serves four very generously.

RICOTTA LASAGNE
Noodle, spinach and cheese in swirls

Lasagne:

2 bunches spinach, finely chopped
2 tablespoons Parmesan cheese
1 cup ricotta cheese

¼ teaspoon nutmeg
salt and pepper to taste
8 boiled lasagne noodles

Steam spinach until it is quite limp over low heat, about 7 minutes. Mix the spinach that is well drained with the cheeses, nutmeg, salt and pepper. Coat each noodle with 2 to 3 tablespoons of the mixture along its entire length, roll up, turn on end so that you see the spiral and place in a shallow baking pan.

Sauce:

2 cups tomato sauce
2 cloves garlic, finely minced
½ cup onions, chopped

½ teaspoon basil
½ teaspoon coarse red pepper
salt and pepper to taste

Mix all of the sauce ingredients together and pour over all rolled-up noodles. Bake at 350 degrees for 35 minutes. Serves four.

TAGLIARINI CON SPARAGI
Egg noodles with asparagus

2 pounds fresh asparagus
4 tablespoons olive oil
2 small cloves garlic, minced
4 cups canned strained plum tomatoes

salt and pepper to taste
1 pound narrow egg noodles
½ cup grated Parmesan cheese

Clean asparagus and remove tough stalks. Cut in half; dry. Heat olive oil in a large saucepan. Add garlic and asparagus; sauté 10 minutes over low flame. Add tomatoes, salt and pepper to taste. Cover and simmer slowly for 1 hour. Stir occasionally to prevent burning. Cook noodles about 12 minutes or until tender in 5 quarts of rapidly boiling salted water. Drain and place on hot platter. Cover with sauce and asparagus. Sprinkle generously with grated Parmesan cheese. Serve very hot. Serves four.

SPAGHETTINI BAGARIA
Eggplant spaghetti

4 tablespoons olive oil
2 cloves garlic, minced
4 cups strained, canned plum tomatoes
salt and pepper to taste
2 tablespoons green olives, chopped
1 tablespoon capers

2 leaves sweet basil, chopped
1 small eggplant, diced
1 pound spaghettini
4 quarts water
½ cup grated Pecorino cheese

Heat olive oil in saucepan and brown garlic. Add tomatoes, salt and pepper to taste. Add olives, capers and basil. Cover pan and simmer over very low heat for 45 minutes. Add diced eggplant and simmer 20 minutes longer or until eggplant is tender. Cook spaghettini 12 minutes in 4 quarts of rapidly boiling salted water. When tender, drain and arrange on hot platter. Pour hot sauce over this and sprinkle with grated Pecorino cheese. Serve very hot. Serves four.

ZUPPA DI LENTICCHI
Lentil soup

1 cup lentils
2 quarts water
1 clove garlic, minced
2 stalks celery, sliced
1 teaspoon parsley, chopped

4 tablespoons olive oil
½ cup tomatoes, chopped
salt and pepper to taste
Romano cheese, grated

Cook lentils in 2 quarts of boiling water for 1 hour. In a saucepan, sauté onion, garlic, celery and parsley in olive oil; cook until slightly browned. Add tomatoes and cook for 10 minutes longer. Pour this mixture into pot with lentils. Salt and pepper to taste. Cover and let simmer for 15 minutes or until lentils are soft. Serve in deep soup bowls and sprinkle with grated Romano cheese if desired. Serves four.

MELENZANA ALLA PARMIGIANA
Eggplant Parmesan

2 tablespoons tomato paste
2½ cups strained canned tomatoes
½ cup olive oil
1 large eggplant
salt and pepper to taste

2 cups bread crumbs
½ cup grated Parmesan cheese
1 tablespoon parsley, chopped
2 cloves garlic, finely minced
½ pound mozzarella cheese

Blend tomato paste with tomatoes. Add 2 tablespoons of olive oil, a pinch of salt and simmer in saucepan for 30 minutes. Slice eggplant crosswise into ½-inch slices. Place in bowl; cover with hot water and let stand for 5 minutes. Drain; dry with absorbent paper. Fry in hot oil about 3 minutes on each side or until soft and light brown. Sprinkle with salt and pepper to taste. Remove from pan. Mix bread crumbs, Parmesan cheese, parsley, garlic, a pinch of salt and pepper. Then place one layer of eggplant in bottom of baking dish; sprinkle with bread crumb mixture; pour some tomato sauce over this. Alternate layers until all ingredients are used. Top with mozzarella sliced thin. Bake for 10 minutes in moderate oven at 350 degrees, or until mozzarella turns slightly brown. Serve very hot. Serves four.

ZUCCHINI E POMODORO
Zucchini with tomatoes

2 pounds zucchini, sliced
4 tablespoons olive or salad oil
1 medium onion, sliced
1 green pepper, sliced

1½ teaspoons salt
¼ teaspoon pepper
3 cups tomato juice

Sauté zucchini in olive oil. Turn when lightly brown. Add onion and green pepper. Season with salt and pepper. After sautéing until soft, add tomato juice. Cook covered over low heat for 40 minutes, or until zucchini are tender and tomato juice forms thick sauce. Serves four.

Mexican

Mexican cooking is a unique blend of Indian and Spanish foods. Mexican cooking starts—now as in Aztec days—with tortillas, the special bread of Mexico. Taken hot off the griddle and folded around cooked beans with an added spoon of chili salsa, the soft tortillas make a hearty and delicious treat. They may also be stuffed or rolled with almost any kind of food that is not too liquid, and then fried. The mainstays of Mexican peasant cooking are corn and chilies. Rice, a principal food of the middle class, is served almost daily at both the noon and evening meals. Nearly every region of Mexico has its own special chilies, with over 140 total varieties. The popular varieties of chilies are readily available and in preparing the traditional Mexican recipes, the amount of chili may be easily altered to personal taste without affecting the fine quality of the dish. In the larger cities of Mexico one finds a more sophisticated and continental cuisine, greatly influenced by French and Spanish cooking. A unique celebration is held in Oaxaca on Christmas eve, called *Noche de Rabanos*, or Radish Night. Big red radishes, plentiful during this season, are cut in fancy shapes and soaked in water overnight. The next day they look like huge fantastic flowers, and are used to decorate the small stands around the main plaza for the celebration.

HUEVOS TOSTADAS
Eggs with cheese and tortillas

4 tablespoons oil
4 corn tortillas (see page 69)
6 eggs
½ cup canned green chili, chopped
4 tablespoons milk
salt and pepper
1 tablespoon butter

1 cup Cheddar or Jack cheese, shredded
½ cup green onions, thinly sliced
1 large avocado, sliced in lengthwise
    strips
2 small tomatoes, cut into wedges
ripe olives
bottled taco sauce

In a small frying pan, heat salad oil over medium heat. Fry one tortilla at a time until it crisps and browns lightly. In a bowl beat eggs lightly. Add green chili, milk, and salt and pepper to taste. Heat the butter in another frying pan and scramble eggs until just softly set. On a large baking sheet, arrange tortillas. Divide and spread scrambled egg on each tortilla, then sprinkle with cheese. Broil about 4 inches below heat, just until cheese is melted. Garnish each tortilla with green onions, avocado slices, tomato wedges and olives. Serve with the taco sauce. Serves four.

QUESO CON AJISES
Cheese and chili casserole

½ cup canned green chilies, chopped
1 pound Cheddar cheese, grated
1 pound Montery Jack cheese, grated
4 eggs
⅔ cup evaporated milk

1 tablespoon flour
½ teaspoon salt
½ teaspoon pepper
2 medium tomatoes, sliced

Combine chopped green chilies and grated cheeses and place in a well-buttered shallow 2-quart casserole. Separate eggs, place the whites in a large bowl and beat until very stiff. Beat egg yolks with evaporated milk, flour, salt and pepper. When smooth, fold the egg whites into the yolk mixture and pour over the cheese in the casserole. Use a fork to "ooze" the egg mixture through the cheese mixture. Bake in a preheated oven at 325 degrees for 30 minutes. Remove casserole, arrange tomato slices on the top and return to the oven for 15 minutes more. Serves four.

RAJAS CON QUESO
Pepper strips with cream cheese

4 large green peppers
4 tomatoes
2 onions, sliced
3 tablespoons oil

¼ cup water
1½ teaspoons salt
8 ounces cream cheese

Arrange green peppers, halved, cut side down on the rack of a preheated broiler and broil them 2 to 3 inches from the heat until the skins start to brown and blister. Cut the peppers lengthwise into ½-inch strips. Plunge tomatoes into a large saucepan of boiling water and let them stand for 2 minutes. Drain the tomatoes, peel and chop them. In a large skillet, sauté onions in oil until they are golden brown. Add the pepper strips, tomatoes, water and salt; cook the mixture over moderately low heat until the liquid comes to a boil. Stir in sliced cream cheese and simmer the mixture, stirring occasionally, for 10 minutes. Serves four.

ENSALADA DE CALABACITAS Y AGUACATE
Zucchini and avocado salad

8 small zucchini squash
2 avocados
1 small onion, chopped
1 stalk celery, chopped
¼ cup olive oil
1 tablespoon wine vinegar

6 fresh mint leaves, chopped
1 clove garlic, minced
1½ teaspoons salt
½ teaspoon pepper
2 hard-boiled eggs, quartered
lettuce leaves

Scrub zucchini, trim the stem ends and halve the zucchini lengthwise. In a saucepan blanch them in enough boiling water to cover for 3 to 4 minutes, or until they are barely tender. Drain the zucchini and scoop out the pulp with a small spoon, being careful not to tear the shells. Dice the pulp and in a bowl combine with avocados which have been peeled, seeded and diced. Add onion and garlic and mix thoroughly. In another bowl mix olive oil, wine vinegar, mint leaves, garlic, salt and pepper. Combine the dressing well and stir it into the avocado mixture. Spoon the mixture into the shells and chill. Arrange the zucchini on a platter lined with lettuce leaves and garnish them with egg quarters. Serves four.

HABAS VERDES CON QUESO
Lima beans with cream cheese

3 cups fresh shelled lima beans
1 onion, minced
2 cloves garlic, minced
2 tablespoons butter
2 tomatoes, peeled and chopped

1 jalapeño chili, seeded and chopped
1½ teaspoons salt
½ teaspoon pepper
8 ounces cream cheese

In a saucepan cook lima beans in enough boiling water to cover for 25 to 30 minutes, or until they are tender. Drain the beans. In a skillet sauté onion and garlic in butter for 2 to 3 minutes. Add chopped tomatoes, chili, salt, pepper and simmer the mixture, stirring occasionally, for 10 minutes. Slice cream cheese and add to the mixture, stirring occasionally, for 5 minutes, or until the cheese is melted. Add lima beans and simmer another 5 minutes. Serves four.

ARROZ CON QUESO
Rice, with beans and cheese

1½ cups brown rice, cooked with salt
1 cup cooked black beans
3 cloves garlic, minced
1 large onion, chopped
½ cup canned chilies, chopped

¾ pound Jack cheese, shredded
½ pound ricotta cheese thinned slightly
   with milk
½ cup Cheddar cheese, grated

Mix rice, beans, garlic, onion, and chilies. Layer this mixture alternately in a greased casserole with the Jack and ricotta cheeses. End with rice mixture. Bake at 350 degrees for 30 minutes. During last few minutes of baking, sprinkle grated Cheddar cheese over the top. Serves four.

ENSALADA DE CHIAPAS
Avocado, banana and celery salad

8 stalks celery
2 tablespoons lemon juice
1½ teaspoons salt
1½ teaspoons sugar
2 avocados

2 bananas
4 tablespoons cream cheese
lettuce leaves
½ cup chopped walnuts

With a vegetable peeler, peel stalks of celery and cut into very thin slices. In a bowl mix the celery with lemon juice, salt and sugar. In another bowl, mash together peeled and seeded avocados, bananas and cream cheese. Combine the mixture with the celery and arrange the salad on a serving plate lined with lettuce leaves. Garnish with the chopped walnuts. Serves four.

TORTILLAS
Flat corn bread

1 cup boiling water
1 cup corn meal

1 teaspoon salt
2 teaspoons shortening

Stir boiling water into corn meal. Add salt and shortening. Mix well. Divide into 12 balls. Pat into very thin cakes. Bake on greased griddle, turning as they brown. Makes one dozen tortillas.

Oriental

"There is no one who does not eat and drink. But few there are who can appreciate taste." This observation was made long ago by Confucius. The essence of Oriental cooking lies in the traditional insistence that food must have flavor even though the ingredients may be common and inexpensive. Oriental cooking in many respects is one of the most unique and economical cuisines of the world. Scarcity of fuel and food shaped this approach to meal preparation. With wood in short supply, the fire used for heating the house was also used for cooking. Today, almost all Oriental home-cooking is done over a single source of heat. The *wok*, a rounded shallow pan with a curved bottom, is the basic cooking utensil. One aspect that distinguishes Oriental cooking from all others is the attention given to the cutting of the ingredients. Whether sliced, diced or shredded, these are cut uniformly so they will cook uniformly. Stir-frying in the *wok* continues to be the most characteristic method of cooking. The point of stir-frying is to keep the food moving constantly so that all parts come in contact with the hottest portion of the pan, and cook quickly and evenly. In this method of preparation, vegetables retain their crisp texture and shape, and their vitamins are not lost in overcooking. These dishes are often seasoned with soy sauce, which is made by a complicated process of fermenting soy beans and toasted wheat. For the Oriental, rice remains the staple of the diet and is considered the staff of life. Leaving a single uneaten grain in the rice bowl is regarded as bad manners.

ORIENTAL

FOO YONG DAHN
Chinese spinach omelets

3 eggs, slightly beaten
½ cup cooked spinach, chopped
½ cup water chestnuts, finely chopped
¼ cup green pepper, finely chopped
¼ cup onion, finely chopped
¼ teaspoon salt
¼ teaspoon pepper

vegetable oil
2 tablespoons butter
4 teaspoons cornstarch
2 teaspoons sugar
1 cup water
3 tablespoons soy sauce

Combine eggs, spinach, water chestnuts, green pepper, onion, salt and pepper. Mix well. Drop from tablespoon onto hot well-oiled griddle. Brown on both sides over medium-high heat. Place on tray and keep warm in oven while preparing sauce. In a saucepan, melt butter and stir in cornstarch, sugar, water and soy sauce. Cook and stir till thickened and bubbly. Pour in small saucedish and pass with Foo Yong Dahn. Makes about 2 dozen small omelets, serving four.

CH'AO PO TS'AI
Chinese spinach with water chestnuts

1 pound fresh spinach
2 tablespoons salad oil
2 tablespoons soy sauce

½ teaspoon sugar
2 tablespoons onion, finely minced
½ cup canned water chestnuts

Wash and pat spinach leaves dry. Remove stems and tear spinach leaves into bite-size pieces. In a large saucepan, simmer spinach with a small amount of water for 3 minutes. Drain thoroughly. In a skillet, heat oil, soy sauce and sugar; add spinach and onion. Cook and toss until spinach is well coated, 2 to 3 minutes. Stir in water chestnuts. Serves four.

SUP KUM CHING CHOY
Chinese bean sprouts, mushrooms, zucchini and carrots

3 tablespoons oil
1 cup carrots, thinly sliced
1 onion, thinly sliced
1 clove garlic, minced
1 large green pepper, cut in thin strips

1 cup zucchini, thinly sliced
1 cup mushrooms, thinly sliced
2 cups bean sprouts
2 to 4 tablespoons soy sauce

In a wok or large frying pan, heat about 1 tablespoon of the oil over high heat; add carrots and cook, stirring for 1 minute. Add the onion, garlic and green pepper and cook, stirring, 1 minute longer. Add more oil as needed to prevent sticking. Add the zucchini and mushrooms and continue to cook about 2 minutes or until all vegetables are just tender. Stir in bean sprouts and heat through. Season to taste with soy sauce. Serves four.

MOYASHI NO GOMA SU AE
Japanese bean sprouts and cucumbers with sesame dressing

1 cup fresh bean sprouts
1 cucumber
2 tablespoons sesame seeds

pinch of sugar
1 teaspoon soy sauce
1 teaspoon rice vinegar

Wash bean sprouts, then quickly plunge them into a kettle of boiling water. Drain immediately. With a vegetable peeler, partially peel cucumber lengthwise, leaving strips of green skin. Cut the cucumber diagonally into ¼-inch slices and cut the slices into ¼-inch strips. Combine the bean sprouts and cucumber in a bowl. Heat a heavy skillet over moderately high heat, add sesame seeds and roast them, shaking the pan constantly until they are lightly colored. Spoon sesame seeds into a mortar and add a pinch of sugar. Grind the sesame seeds coarsely and add soy sauce and rice vinegar. Grind the mixture for a few seconds, or until it is well blended. Gently toss the cucumber and bean sprouts with the dressing. Serves four.

NAMUL
Korean watercress salad-relish

2 bunches watercress
2 green onions and tops, chopped
¼ teaspoon pepper
¾ teaspoon salt
1½ teaspoons sugar

2 tablespoons soy sauce
1½ tablespoons vinegar
¼ teaspoon crushed red pepper
2 teaspoons toasted sesame seeds

Wash watercress; drain, then cut into 2-inch lengths. Mix together the green onions, pepper, salt, sugar, soy sauce, vinegar and crushed red pepper. Pour over watercress, then sprinkle with sesame seeds. Chill or serve at room temperature. Serves four.

SAYUR GÒDÒK
Indonesian asparagus and bamboo shoots with coconut milk

4 tablespoons oil
4 tablespoons chopped onion
½ teaspoon red pepper flakes
1 teaspoon cardamon
2 tablespoons peanut butter
2 teaspoons coriander

1 teaspoon salt
2 tablespoons lemon juice
2 cups coconut milk
2 pounds asparagus, cut in 2-inch
  lengths
1 cup bamboo shoots

In a wok or large frying pan, heat oil slightly and add onion; cook until lightly browned. Add red pepper flakes, cardamon, peanut butter, coriander, salt, lemon juice, coconut milk and stir well. Add asparagus and bamboo shoots and cook until asparagus is tender. Serves four.

PETJEL
Indonesian cooked vegetable salad with peanut sauce

4 cups various cooked vegetables
4 hard-boiled eggs
½ cup fried peanuts, roughly ground,
  or 6 tablespoons crunchy peanut
  butter

1½ teaspoons chili powder
1 clove garlic, finely minced
1 onion, finely minced
1 tablespoon brown sugar
⅔ cup water

Arrange on a plate, small separate heaps of lightly cooked vegetables, such as shredded cabbage, spinach, bean sprouts, green beans and sliced potatoes. Halve hard-boiled eggs and arrange by vegetables. In a blender, combine peanuts or peanut butter, chili powder, garlic, onion, brown sugar and water. Blend thoroughly and pour in a small bowl. Serve vegetables at room temperature accompanied by the bowl of sauce. Serves four.

Romanian

The complicated culinary heritage of Romania is interwoven with a history of invasion and conquest. Romania is an ancient country and its cooking reflects a blend of Europe and the Middle East. However one dish, *mamaliga*, remains outstandingly Romanian, serving as the staple of working men and a favorite with all economic classes. It is a mush of corn meal, eaten plain with melted butter or topped with a poached egg and sprinkled with cheese. Romanians have a tremendous love for fresh vegetables, combined in unusual concoctions and artfully enhanced with herbs. In order that fresh vegetables will be available during winter, the peasant places them with leaves and straw in a deep hole in the ground, and the snow cover preserves their freshness. This method is preferred to canning. In Romania, sassafras is used not only to flavor stews and soups, but the peasants also tie a bit of this herb around the baby's wrist since infants love to suck on it. Love of good food has become a national trait, and the people believe enjoyment of food is partly a matter of early training. The Romanian mother makes a steeped liquid of herbs and sours it a little by adding lemon juice, raspberries or grapes. She places this in a little earthen jar and moistens her baby's lips with the liquid, acquainting the child with beautiful aromas and fine tastes at a very early age.

ROMANIAN

VINETE CU USTUROI
Stuffed eggplant

2 eggplants
1 large onion, sliced
olive oil
1 cup diced mixed vegetables: such as
  celery, carrots, turnips, parsley and
  green leeks

2 tomatoes, sliced
1 cup tomato sauce
2 cloves garlic, crushed
parsley, finely chopped
salt and pepper

Wash eggplants and cut lengthwise into halves. Scoop out the pulp. To prepare filling, sauté onions in oil until soft. Add cup of diced mixed vegetables. Scald and chop eggplant pulp, then combine with vegetables and fried onions. Fry until brown. Stuff this mixture into the eggplant hollows, arrange the eggplant halves nicely in a baking dish, cover with tomato slices and sprinkle with olive oil. Bake in a moderate oven, 350 degrees for about 35 minutes. During the baking, baste with tomato sauce, in which the crushed cloves of garlic have been placed to soak. When done, remove from the oven and sprinkle with finely chopped parsley. Salt and pepper to taste. Delicious served with small sharp red peppers. Serves four.

SUPA DE CHIMEN
Caraway seed soup with dumplings

Soup:

2 quarts cold water
¼ cup caraway seeds
2 large onions
salt and pepper

2 tablespoons butter
1 tablespoon green scallions, chopped
sprig of parsley, chopped
1 tablespoon flour

Add to cold water: the caraway seeds, onions—washed with the peel left on—and salt and pepper to taste. Boil until tender. Now fry in a deep iron pan the butter, finely chopped green scallions and parsley; simmer until soft. Put in one tablespoonful of flour, stirring constantly until it becomes a nice dark brown. Add some of the boiling caraway water slowly, with constant stirring, until you get a thick sauce. Cook slowly for 10 minutes, then pour it over the boiling caraway seeds and again cook on low heat for 10 minutes. Strain the soup into another pot, pressing the ingredients through a sieve, and bring to a boil.

Dumplings:

1 egg
cold water
1 tablespoon olive oil

pinch of salt
flour

Beat together quickly with a spoon: the egg, half an eggshell full of cold water, olive oil, salt and enough flour to make a soft dough. Place the dough on a wooden board, and with a knife wetted in the soup, cut off small pieces and drop into the soup. Boil until done, about 10 minutes. This soup is an aid to good digestion. Serves four.

PRAZ UMPLUT CU OREZI
Leeks stuffed with rice

4 large leeks
2 onions, finely chopped
2 tablespoons olive oil
1 cup uncooked rice
vegetable bouillon
salt and pepper
dash of thyme
flour

1 tablespoon butter
breadcrumbs
½ cup tomato sauce
½ teaspoon sugar
juice of ½ lemon
¼ cup parsley, finely chopped

Cut off the white part of leeks to about finger lengths. Scald in salted water and drain. Without tearing, slip off the shells. These leek tubes are used to hold the stuffing. Prepare the stuffing by frying onion in olive oil. Add rice and continue frying. Now slowly add cold water until the rice is covered. Cook until the water is absorbed. Cover again with vegetable bouillon, add salt and pepper to taste and sprinkle with a little thyme. Cook until done with the liquid absorbed. Cool, then fill the leek tubes with stuffing. Dip the ends in flour and fry in hot oil very slightly. Grease the bottom and sides of a casserole with the butter and sprinkle with bread crumbs. Place the stuffed leeks carefully inside, pour over the top a mixture of tomato sauce, sugar and juice of lemon. Sprinkle with parsley, cover and bake in a moderate oven about 30 minutes. Serves four.

ATUAT DE VIN
Apricots in wine batter

8 egg yolks
½ cup brown sugar
grated vanilla bark

2 cups flour
¾ cup white wine
fresh apricots or any fresh fruit

Beat together very well in a bowl: egg yolks, sugar and a little grated vanilla bark. Add flour, mix well and then thin very slowly with tablespoons of good white wine. Pit apricots, dry, soak well in the batter and fry in very hot and deep sweet butter. Serve hot. Serves four.

TOCANA DE CARTOFI
Potato stew

6 medium potatoes, peeled
water
2 onions, finely chopped
2 tablespoons butter
1 tablespoon flour
salt and pepper
paprika

1 cup mixture of chopped parsley,
  fennel and celery
2 cups tomato juice
1 green pepper, diced
½ cup sour cream

Cut each potato lengthwise into 4 slices and keep in cold water in a bowl. In a deep frying pan, sauté onions in butter until lightly browned. Add flour and mix constantly until brown. Add slowly a little water to make a thin sauce; add salt and pepper, a dash of red paprika and let simmer slowly. Add parsley, fennel and celery mixture to frying pan. Let cook for a little while on low heat. Now add the potatoes, pour tomato juice over them, and cook until the potatoes are done. If necessary, add more tomato juice. When the potatoes are done, add green pepper and cook 5 minutes more. About ½ cup of liquid should remain at the end. Serve hot. Add 2 tablespoons of sour cream for each serving, and garnish by sprinkling with chopped parsley. Serves four.

VINETE CU BRINZA
Eggplant, cheese and egg sandwiches

1 large eggplant
salt and pepper
flour
butter

2 egg yolks
½ cup Parmesan cheese, grated
oil
2 tablespoons parsley, finely chopped

Cut eggplant lengthwise into rather thick slices. Sprinkle with a little salt and pepper, then dip in flour and pat in well. Sear quickly in hot butter and remove to a plate. Place the slices adjacent to each other; do not pile one on top of the other. Let stand while you prepare a thick paste out of egg yolks and cheese. Spread this thickly on the eggplant slices, then join two slices together to form sandwiches. Let stand until you are ready to serve, then dip both sides in hot butter, place quickly into a frying pan and fry in deep hot oil. Remove the eggplant sandwiches with a spatula and let drain. Very quickly sauté the parsley in a little butter and sprinkle over the eggplant. Serve very hot. Serves four.

Russian

In the beginning, Russian cuisine—like all other early cooking—was based on grains and cereals, especially those that could withstand the severe climate. Dark, coarse-grained breads made with rye have been the most important food of Russia throughout history. Buckwheat groats, cooked into a porridge called *kasha*, became a Russian staple centuries ago, and are eaten daily in various forms at different meals. The Russians have learned to rely on those vegetables that could be grown during the short summer season, and would also preserve well for winter use. These root vegetables became traditional ingredients for their hearty soups. Beets, cabbage, carrots, turnips and potatoes are often used in Russian cooking. The people also became experts in the art of pickling, and no meal is complete without such dishes as pickled mushrooms or cucumbers. Today Russian cuisine offers some exotic and exciting contrasts, with each of the fifteen republics providing a distinct style of fare. Gradually the exchange of foods and recipes within the country has increased, and cooking has become more versatile with a greater range of available ingredients. Food remains an important part of any holiday, and of all celebrations in the Russian Orthodox Church, Easter is the most traditionally observed. Eggs are decorated and dyed in intricate and colorful designs for this occasion. The association of eggs and Easter is an ancient one; the egg has been a symbol of new life since pre-Christian times.

RUSSIAN

BORSCHT
Cold beet soup

2 cups raw beets, grated
water
juice of 2 lemons
2 tablespoons sugar

½ teaspoon salt
2 eggs, beaten
sour cream

Cover beets with water and cook until tender. Add lemon juice, sugar, salt and stir. Add a little beet broth to eggs. Stir until well blended. Add eggs to beet broth. Cool. Serve cold with sour cream. It is often served with hot boiled potatoes in cold soup. Serves four.

AGURKAI SU RUKCSCIA GRIETNE
Cucumber, egg, and sour cream salad

Salad:

4 medium cucumbers
2 tablespoons salt
½ teaspoon white vinegar

4 large lettuce leaves
1 tablespoon fresh dill leaves, finely
cut

Dressing:

3 hard-boiled eggs
1 teaspoon prepared mustard
⅓ cup sour cream

2 teaspoons white wine vinegar
¼ teaspoon sugar
¼ teaspoon white pepper

Peel, halve and cut the cucumbers crosswise into ½-inch-thick slices. In a mixing bowl, combine the cucumber slices, salt and vinegar, and toss them about with a large spoon until the cucumber is well moistened. Marinate at room temperature for 30 minutes, then drain the cucumbers through a sieve and pat them thoroughly dry with paper towels. Place them in a large mixing bowl. Separate the yolks from the whites of the hard-boiled eggs. Cut the whites into strips ⅛-inch wide and 1- to 2-inches long, and stir the egg whites into the cucumber. With the back of a large spoon, rub the egg yolks through fine sieve set over a small bowl. Slowly beat in the mustard, sour cream, vinegar, sugar and white pepper. When the dressing is smooth, pour it over the cucumbers and toss together gently but thoroughly. Taste for seasoning. To serve, arrange the lettuce leaves on a large flat serving plate or on individual plates and mound the salad on top of them. Sprinkle with dill and refrigerate until ready to serve. Serves four.

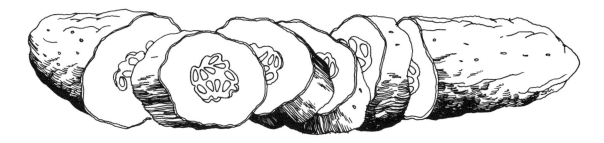

MEDIVNYK
Spiced honey cake

¾ cup honey
½ teaspoon cinnamon
¼ teaspoon cloves
¼ teaspoon nutmeg
1 teaspoon baking soda
4 tablespoons butter, softened
½ cup dark brown sugar
3 eggs, separated

2 cups flour
¼ teaspoon salt
1 teaspoon baking powder
10 tablespoons raisins
6 tablespoons dried currants
½ cup walnuts, finely chopped
3 tablespoons butter, softened

In a saucepan bring the honey to a boil over moderate heat, stirring almost constantly. Stir in the cinnamon, cloves, nutmeg and baking soda and set aside to cool to room temperature. In a large bowl, cream the butter and sugar until light and fluffy. Beat in egg yolks, one at a time, and stir in the cooled, spiced honey. Combine 1¾ cups of the flour with the salt and baking powder, and beat into the sugar and egg mixture. Combine the raisins, currants and walnuts and toss together with remaining ¼ cup of flour; fold this into the batter. Preheat oven to 300 degrees. Beat the egg whites in a large bowl until they form stiff peaks on the beater when lifted out of the bowl. Gently fold the egg whites into the batter. Coat the bottom and sides of a 9 × 5 × 3-inch loaf pan with 2 tablespoons of the softened butter. Line the inside of loaf pan with brown paper, and with remaining 1 tablespoon of butter. Pour the batter into the pan and bake in center of the oven for 1½ hours, or until a toothpick inserted into the center of the cake comes out clean. With a knife, loosen the sides of the cake from the pan and invert the cake onto a rack. Let the cake cool to room temperature, then cover loosely with wax paper and set aside for 1 or 2 days to allow the flavor to develop properly.

NON
Flat onion bread

6 tablespoons butter	1 teaspoon salt
1½ cups onions, finely chopped	2½ to 3 cups flour
¾ cup lukewarm water	

Melt 1 tablespoon of the butter in a heavy skillet set over high heat. Add the onions, reduce the heat to low and—stirring constantly—cook 3 to 5 minutes, or until the onions are soft but not brown. Transfer them to a bowl and cool to room temperature. Melt the remaining 5 tablespoons of butter in the skillet and pour it into a large mixing bowl. Add the lukewarm water and with a large spoon, stir in the chopped onions, salt and 2½ cups of the flour—½ cup at a time. If necessary, beat in as much of the remaining ½ cup of flour as you need to make a dough that does not stick to your fingers. Gather the dough into a large, compact ball and divide it into 16 pieces. With the palms of your hands, shape each piece of dough into a 1½- to 2-inch ball. Then, with a lightly floured rolling pin, roll out the balls one at a time into circles that are about 8 inches in diameter. Set the rounds of dough aside. Set a heavy 10- to 12-inch ungreased pan over high heat. When it is hot enough for a drop of water flicked across its surface to instantly evaporate, place one round of dough in the center. Brown for 3 or 4 minutes on each side, turning it over with a wide spatula; do not be concerned if the bread does not brown evenly. Cool on a rack. If the bread becomes limp after a day or so, place the rounds in a single layer on a cookie sheet and bake them for 5 to 10 minutes in a preheated 300-degree oven to freshen. Makes 16 breads.

Scandinavian

As far as food is concerned, the Scandinavian countries share a special culinary tradition, with recipes and customs intermingled. The natural taste is characteristic, simple, and not highly spiced. In dishes requiring an assertive contrast, a little chopped onion or parsley, horseradish, mustard, pickled beet, or cucumber is used. Scandinavian bread is still one of the most varied foods, appearing in many shapes, textures, and consistencies. Some, made without leavening, become flat disks, as was the first bread of the area. After baking these were allowed to dry out naturally, then were pierced to string on stakes, and suspended from the ceiling. This unusual preparation of bread was a result of their short Northern growing season, which forced the harvest of immature grain. Storage of green grain would have caused it to spoil, so they ground the kernels immediately into bread. The Scandinavians take the pleasure of eating very seriously, and have faithfully preserved the tradition that every festivity keeps a distinct menu. Christmas, the major celebration of the year, has a special significance for Scandinavians. Even in pagan times, a midwinter festival was held during this, the darkest period of the year. On Christmas eve, a rice porridge is traditionally served. Custom demands that an unpeeled almond be placed in the porridge. The person who gets this almond in his portion is said to be the one to marry during the following year, a superstition which occurs in many countries in different forms.

SCANDINAVIAN

LANTTULAATIKKO
Turnip pie

2 pounds yellow turnip
½ teaspoon salt
water
1½ cups fine dry bread crumbs
1 cup half and half

1 tablespoon sugar
dash ground white pepper
⅛ teaspoon ground nutmeg
2 eggs, lightly beaten
2 tablespoons butter

Cook turnip that has been peeled and cut into ½-inch cubes in just enough salted water to cover until tender, about 30 minutes. Drain and mash. Stir in 1 cup of the bread crumbs, half and half, sugar, pepper and nutmeg. Taste and salt, if needed. Stir in beaten eggs. Use part of the butter to grease a 9-inch round cake tin, about 2 inches deep. Coat with 1 to 2 tablespoons of the remaining crumbs. Spread turnip mixture in pan, sprinkle with remaining crumbs and dot with remaining butter. Bake in a slow oven at 325 degrees for 1 hour, or until lightly browned. Serves four.

PÄHKINÄ-PAISTI
Rice and nut steak

1 cup bread crumbs
1½ cups heavy cream
⅓ cup melted butter
2 cups cooked rice
1 cup ground nuts

1 teaspoon salt
¼ teaspoon pepper
3 eggs, well beaten
1 egg yolk

Soak the bread crumbs in the cream for 5 minutes. Add butter, rice, nuts, salt, pepper, 3 eggs, and beat well. Pour into a buttered 10-inch loaf pan. Brush the top thoroughly with the egg yolk. Bake in a 350-degree oven for 1 hour. Cut into ¾-inch slices and serve. Serves four.

SIENIMUREKE
Mushroom casserole

3 tablespoons butter
2 small onions, chopped
2 eggs
⅔ cup dry bread crumbs
¾ cup milk

¾ cup half and half
2 teaspoons salt
¼ teaspoon pepper
1 pound fresh mushrooms, coarsely
  chopped

Melt butter in medium skillet, add onions and sauté until golden. Meanwhile, in a greased 1½-quart casserole beat eggs, then mix in bread crumbs, milk, half and half, salt and pepper until the liquid is absorbed. Blend in mushrooms and onions. Bake at 350 degrees for about an hour or until golden brown and set. Serves four.

RAKOSTKABARET
Raw vegetable medley

1 cup cabbage, finely shredded
2 cooked beets, coarsely grated
2 carrots, coarsely grated
1 apple, peeled and grated

1 tablespoon lemon juice
½ cup mayonnaise
2 tablespoons milk

Combine cabbage, beets, carrots, and grated apple. Mix in lemon juice. Blend mayonnaise with milk; add to vegetables and toss to mix well. Serves four.

KLAPPGRÖOT
Whipped farina

2½ cups water
1 can frozen concentrate for punch,
6 ounces

4 tablespoons farina

In a saucepan, combine water and punch concentrate; bring to a boil. Sprinkle farina into boiling mixture; stir vigorously. Simmer over low heat until farina is cooked, about 5 minutes. Pour mixture into a bowl and beat with an egg beater for about 1 minute at a time, at intervals of about 5 minutes, until pudding is fluffy and cool. Chill. Serve with cream if desired. Serves four.

AEBLESUPPE
Apple soup

5 medium apples, unpeeled
4 cups water
½ teaspoon lemon rind, grated
2 tablespoons cornstarch

¼ cup cold water
½ cup white wine
⅔ cup brown sugar
1 teaspoon cinnamon

Quarter unpeeled apples, simmer in water with grated lemon rind for 5 minutes. Add cornstarch to ¼ cup cold water and dissolve; add to the apple broth stirring constantly. Add wine, sugar and cinnamon; simmer an additional 10 minutes. Serve hot or cold. Serves four.

SPINAT OG AEG
Danish eggs on spinach with cheese sauce

6 tablespoons butter
2 bunches spinach, cleaned and well
    drained
salt and pepper
6 tablespoons grated Parmesan cheese

4 eggs
2 tablespoons flour
1½ cups milk
2 tablespoons breadcrumbs

In a saucepan melt 4 tablespoons butter, and stir in spinach. Sauté until wilted. Season to taste with salt and pepper. Spoon into a shallow oven dish. Make 4 hollows by pressing with a spoon and sprinkle hollows with 3 tablespoons of grated cheese. Break an egg into each hollow. To make sauce, melt 1 tablespoon butter in saucepan and stir in flour. Add milk gradually, stirring vigorously. Season to taste with salt and pepper. Simmer for 10 minutes. Remove from heat and add 1 tablespoon butter and 3 tablespoons grated cheese. Spoon sauce gently over eggs and spinach. Sprinkle with breadcrumbs and bake in a preheated oven at 475 degrees for about 10 minutes or until golden brown. Serves four.

Spanish

Spanish food, like that of most countries, varies greatly from region to region, primarily because of climate and geography. Spanish cooking is uncomplicated, depending for its flavor on the freshness of the ingredients and a gentle use of seasonings. The people tend to shy away from piquant foods, and recipes are never spiced to alter basic tastes, but simply to enhance them. The origins of the authentic regional dishes that constitute Spanish cuisine are humble. They began with fishermen and peasants, who combined the products at hand in pots such as earthenware casseroles. A revolution in Spanish cooking was caused by the introduction of the tomato, the pepper and the potato from America in the sixteenth century. In time, these became basic elements of Spanish cuisine. It is natural that olive oil should be used liberally in the cooking, since Spain leads all countries in its production. Nutritionally, olive oil is a desirable addition because it contains no cholesterol and is one of the most easily digested fats. Garlic, used in slowly cooked sauces, is another basic component, contributing gently to the final flavor without seeming offensive. The foundation of countless Spanish sauces is traditionally enhanced with saffron and paprika, in addition to the common use of tomatoes, onion and olive oil. Almonds play an important role in Spanish food. They are served as appetizers, or crushed and added to sauces, and deliciously enrich many desserts and pastries.

REMOLACHA EN VINO TINTO
Beets in Burgundy wine

6 medium-sized whole beets
2 tablespoons olive oil
1 tablespoon butter
1 medium onion, thinly sliced in rings
1 tablespoon flour
¼ cup blanched almonds, slivered

½ cup Burgundy wine
½ cup water
2 tablespoons brown sugar
½ teaspoon salt
1 tablespoon wine vinegar

Cook beets whole, about 30 minutes. Drain and cut off roots and stems. Remove skin; slice thin and place in buttered shallow casserole. In a skillet, heat oil and butter. Add onion rings and sauté until just transparent. Remove with slotted spoon, being careful not to break the rings. Scatter rings over the beets in casserole. To the drippings in skillet, stir in the flour. When the flour is bubbly and golden, add the almonds and sauté 2 or 3 minutes longer. Remove skillet from heat. Combine wine, water, sugar, salt and vinegar. Mix well and slowly add to the skillet, stirring until smooth. Return to heat and cook until thickened. Pour mixture over beets and onion rings in casserole. Cover casserole and simmer over direct heat for about 20 minutes. Serve hot. Serves four.

GAZPACHO
Cold tomato soup

1 cup Sauterne or other white wine
2½ cups tomato juice
1 cup fresh tomatoes, peeled and diced
⅓ cup cucumber, peeled and diced
⅓ cup green pepper, chopped
2 tablespoons parsley, finely chopped

2 tablespoons lemon juice
1 teaspoon instant minced onion
¼ cup ripe olives, chopped
1 teaspoon basil
1 clove garlic, crushed
salt to taste

Chill wine and tomato juice. Combine with all other ingredients and mix well. Serve in large soup bowls with a chunk of ice in each bowl. It's an ideal soup on a hot summer day. Serves four.

BAMIES LADERES
Okra with tomatoes

4 tablespoons olive oil
1 medium onion, chopped
4 large tomatoes, chopped
¼ cup parsley, chopped
salt and pepper

1½ pounds baby okra, tops snipped off
juice of 1 lemon
½ teaspoon ground red pepper
 (optional)

Heat oil and add onions; sauté until tender. Add tomatoes, parsley, salt and pepper to taste and simmer 10 minutes. Add okra, lemon juice and red pepper, and cook covered over low heat until okra is tender, about 40 minutes. Do not stir; shake pan now and then to prevent sticking. Serves four.

FRIJOLES NEGROS
Black bean soup

1 pound black beans
water
2 tablespoons olive oil
1 medium ripe tomato
1 bay leaf
½ medium onion, chopped
½ green pepper, chopped

1 garlic clove, minced
1 teaspoon oregano
¼ teaspoon cumin
2 tablespoons wine vinegar
½ teaspoon hot sauce
2 tablespoons dry sherry
1 tablespoon salt

Wash beans and discard imperfect ones. Place in a deep bowl and cover with 2 inches of water. Soak overnight. The next day, pour beans into a 3- to 4-quart soup kettle with same soaking water. If necessary, add more water so that beans will be covered by 1 inch of liquid. Add remaining ingredients except salt and cook slowly until beans are almost tender about 1 hour. Add salt and simmer until beans are done. Taste and salt, if needed. Serves four.

ENSALADA DE ARROZ
Rice and tomato salad

2 cups rice, cooked
2 green peppers, finely sliced
2 pimentos, finely sliced
4 tomatoes, peeled and cubed
2 tablespoons chopped onion
2 tablespoons chopped parsley

¾ cup olive oil
¼ cup wine vinegar
1½ teaspoons salt
½ teaspoon pepper
1 clove garlic, minced

Combine the cooked rice, green peppers, pimentos, tomatoes, onion and parsley in a bowl. Mix lightly with two forks. Beat together the olive oil, wine vinegar, salt, pepper and garlic. Pour over the rice mixture and again toss lightly. Chill and serve very cold. Serves four.

SALSA COLORADA
Tomato and almond sauce

3 tomatoes
1 clove garlic
½ teaspoon chili pepper
2 yolks of hard-boiled eggs

12 almonds, peeled and toasted
¾ cup olive oil
¼ cup wine vinegar
salt to taste

Bake unpeeled tomatoes and garlic in oven until tomatoes are very soft. Remove peel from tomatoes and garlic, and mash insides in mortar or electric blender with pepper. Add egg yolks and almonds and blend well. Gradually mix in oil and vinegar, season to taste with salt. This sauce is excellent on most steamed or boiled vegetables. Makes 1½ cups sauce.

TARTA DE DÁTILES
Date, fig and walnut pie

8 ounces dates, pitted and chopped
5 dried figs, chopped
⅓ cup walnuts, chopped
7 tablespoons sugar
1½ cups milk
¼ cup cognac
2 egg yolks

3 tablespoons cornstarch
½ teaspoon vanilla
1 baked pastry shell, 9-inch (see
    page 39)
juice of 1 lemon
½ cup candied orange peel, chopped

In a saucepan mix together the dates, figs, walnuts, 2 tablespoons of the sugar, ½ cup of the milk and cognac. Place over low heat and stir constantly until the mixture is well blended. In another saucepan combine egg yolks, 5 tablespoons sugar, cornstarch, vanilla and whisk together until well blended. Gradually add 1 cup milk and whisk until smooth. Cook over low heat, stirring constantly until thickened. Spread this sauce in the pie shell and cover with the date mixture. Sprinkle with lemon juice and top with the orange peel. Bake for 10 minutes in a preheated 350-degree oven. Cool before serving and, if desired, serve with whipped cream or ice cream. Makes one 9-inch pie.

United States

From around the world, people emigrated to the United States, bringing with them the eating habits of their native lands. The immigrant mother, wanting to prepare the foods her family had enjoyed, continued the customs of the past. As the immigrants settled in various parts of the United States, interesting regional foods were developed. Early British settlers established a style of cooking in New England, the French contributed to the Creole cuisine of Louisiana, and the Spaniards and Mexicans to the foods of the Southwest. Scandinavians brought their style of cooking to the North Central United States, and Germans developed a Pennsylvania Dutch cuisine. In the South "soul food" emerged, influenced by the African, American Indian and European peoples. In the Northwestern region, large settlements of Japanese and Scandinavians provided varied and interesting foods, as did the Chinese in San Francisco. In Idaho, the Basque and Welsh made unique contributions to the cooking. Today, throughout the United States one can enjoy varieties of the Mexican taco, the Jewish bagel with cream cheese, the Italian pizza, and this country's version of Oriental cooking—chop suey. Probably the most ethnic and popular foods of the United States are fried chicken, corn-on-the-cob and apple pie. The people of this nation can consider themselves fortunate to have more international flavor in their daily meals than most countries. The old adage seems to fit very well here—that good food knows no boundaries.

UNITED STATES

CHEDDAR ASPARAGUS ROLL-UPS

20 asparagus spears
water
½ pound sharp Cheddar cheese
1 loaf sliced sandwich bread
¾ cup soft butter

1 tablespoon chopped parsley
½ teaspoon dill weed
3 tablespoons sliced green onion
salt and pepper

Discard white fibrous ends of asparagus, and rinse spears. Bring about 1 inch of water to boil in a wide shallow pan; drop in asparagus and boil uncovered until just tender when pierced, about 4 to 7 minutes. Drain well. Cut cheese into sticks about 3 inches long and ½-inch in diameter. Trim crusts from 20 bread slices and flatten each slice slightly with a rolling pin. Combine ½ cup of the butter, parsley, dill, green onion, and salt and pepper to taste. Spread evenly over one side of each bread slice and top each with an asparagus spear and a cheese stick. Roll each slice, secure with a wooden pick and arrange on a baking sheet. Melt the remaining ¼ cup of butter and brush evenly over rolls. Broil 5 inches from heat until golden, about 3 to 5 minutes. Makes 20 rolls.

BLACK-EYED PEAS AND AVOCADO

1½ cups dried black-eyed peas
1 quart water
1½ teaspoons salt
1½ quarts water
1 small onion, chopped

6 tablespoons butter
½ cup rice
1 avocado
½ cup Cheddar cheese, shredded

Wash and rinse peas. Place peas, 1 quart water and ½ teaspoon of the salt in large pan. Bring to a boil and boil 2 minutes covered. Let stand, covered, overnight. Drain peas. Combine remaining salt and 1½ quarts water and bring to a boil. Add drained peas and cover, simmering until tender, about 25 minutes. Brown onions in butter. Drain peas reserving 2½ cups of the liquid. Blend rice, peas, reserved pea liquid, browned onions and butter in a 2-quart saucepan. Cover and simmer 45 minutes or until rice is done. Add more water if needed. Just before serving, peel and dice avocado. Blend avocado and cheese into mixture. Serve at once. Serves four.

BROCCOLI CUSTARD

2 pounds broccoli, cut in 2-inch pieces
    and cooked till tender but crisp
4 eggs, beaten
2 cups cottage cheese, creamed
1 cup corn
⅓ cup green onions, chopped

1 cup Cheddar cheese, shredded
dash hot pepper sauce
salt and pepper
¼ cup butter
⅔ cup seasoned bread crumbs

Place the broccoli in a greased 11 × 7 × 2-inch dish. Combine eggs and cottage cheese in a large bowl and mix well. Add corn, onion, cheese, hot pepper sauce, salt and pepper to taste. Pour over the broccoli. Melt butter and combine with bread crumbs. Sprinkle over top of the casserole and bake at 325 degrees for 45 minutes. Serves four.

CARROT NUT LOAF WITH CHEESE SAUCE

Loaf:

10 medium carrots, sliced
boiling salted water
3 eggs, well-beaten
2 cups milk
½ cup onion, chopped
½ teaspoon sage
1 teaspoon Worcestershire sauce

1 tablespoon prepared mustard
2 tablespoons butter, melted
2 cups dry bread crumbs
1 teaspoon salt
dash of pepper
1 cup walnuts, chopped

Cook carrots in boiling, salted water until tender; drain and mash. Combine all ingredients and mix thoroughly. Pack into a buttered loaf pan; bake at 350 degrees for about 1 hour. Unmold on platter and serve with cheese sauce.

Cheese sauce:

3 tablespoons butter
3 tablespoons flour
½ teaspoon dry mustard
dash of salt

dash of cayenne pepper
2 cups milk
½ cup Cheddar cheese, shredded

Melt butter, stir in flour, dry mustard, salt and cayenne pepper. Add milk gradually and cook slowly until thickened. Add cheese and salt, and stir until cheese is melted.

BRANDIED WALNUT CARROTS

6 carrots
water
¼ cup brandy
½ cup walnuts, chopped

salt and pepper
1 tablespoon butter
parsley, chopped

Peel and slice carrots diagonally. Add enough water with brandy to barely cover carrots. Add butter, and salt and pepper to taste. Cover and cook until liquid is absorbed and carrots are crisp but tender. Toss with walnuts and sprinkle with parsley. Serves four.

CAULIFLOWER CHEESE SOUP

1 medium head cauliflower
4 tablespoons butter
2 tablespoons minced onion
2 tablespoons flour

4 cups milk
1 teaspoon salt
dash of pepper
1 cup sharp Cheddar cheese, shredded

Cook cauliflower and force through a sieve or mash. Set aside. Melt butter, add onion and cook until tender but not browned. Stir in flour; add milk and cauliflower. Stir until smooth and thickened, then stir in salt and pepper. Add ⅔ cup cheese and stir until cheese is melted. Ladle into warm soup bowls and sprinkle with remaining ⅓ cup of cheese. Serves four.

LENTIL AND WALNUT HORS D'OEUVRE BALLS
Lentils, walnuts and carrots

1 cup lentils
4 cups water
1 teaspoon salt
¾ cup walnuts, finely chopped; plus
  more for rolling

⅔ cup carrots, grated
¼ cup onion, minced
1 egg, lightly beaten
salt and pepper to taste

In a large saucepan combine lentils, water and salt. Bring to a boil over moderately high heat; reduce the heat and simmer the lentils, covered, for 45 minutes or until they are soft. Drain the lentils in a sieve and put them through the medium disk of a food mill into a bowl (or use blender). Add ¾ cup walnuts, carrots, onions, egg, and salt and pepper to taste. Combine the mixture well; form heaping teaspoons of the mixture into balls and roll the balls in additional finely chopped walnuts. Chill the balls on a plate, covered, for 1 hour. Roll the balls a second time in the chopped walnuts and fry in deep oil at 360 degrees, a few at a time until they are golden. Transfer the balls with a slotted spoon to paper towels to drain. Serve hot. Makes about 24 hors d'oeuvres.

PRUNE AND NOODLE BAKE

1½ cups noodles
2 eggs, separated
½ cup milk
2½ teaspoons melted butter
½ teaspoon salt

¼ teaspoon pepper
⅛ teaspoon paprika
½ cup Parmesan or Cheddar cheese, grated
1 cup pitted prunes, snipped

Cook noodles according to package directions and drain. Beat egg yolks lightly with milk, butter, salt, pepper, paprika and cheese. Pour over noodles. Add prunes and toss to combine. Beat egg whites until stiff but not dry. Fold lightly into noodle mixture. Pour into a greased 1-quart casserole. Place casserole in pan of water and bake at 350 degrees for 35 minutes, until lightly browned. Serves four.

OATMEAL-DATE PIE

¼ cup soft butter
1 cup honey
3 eggs
⅛ teaspoon salt

1 teaspoon vanilla
1¼ cups rolled oats
¾ cup pitted dates, snipped
9-inch pie shell, optional (see page 39)

Beat the butter and honey together until creamy; add the eggs and beat until smooth. Stir in the salt, vanilla, rolled oats and dates. This mixture may be poured into an unbaked 9-inch pie shell and baked in a 350-degree oven for 45 minutes or until center is set when lightly touched. Let cool completely before cutting. Top each serving with ice cream if you wish. For individual servings, pour the pie filling mixture into 6 greased custard cups. Pour about 1 inch hot water in a baking pan; set custard cups in the water and bake uncovered in a 325-degree oven for 40 minutes, or until set when lightly touched. Excellent change of pace served with light cream for breakfast.

BLUE CHEESE YOGURT DRESSING

1 cup yogurt
1 clove garlic, crushed
¼ teaspoon dry mustard

1½ teaspoons wine vinegar
¼ cup blue cheese, crumbled

Blend yogurt, garlic, mustard and vinegar lightly but thoroughly. Add cheese. Chill at least 30 minutes before using. Serve over lettuce wedges, mixed greens or fruit salads. Makes just over one cup.

ZESTY YOGURT DRESSING

1 cup yogurt
2 tablespoons lemon juice
1 tablespoon onion, chopped

¼ teaspoon salt
¼ teaspoon sugar

Combine yogurt, lemon juice, onion, salt and sugar in a bowl and beat well. Store in a covered jar and refrigerate. Shake well before using. Serve with green salad. Makes just over one cup.

LETTUCE-SESAME SALAD

2 bunches Boston lettuce
¼ cup water chestnuts, thinly sliced
4 tablespoons toasted sesame seeds
¼ cup Parmesan cheese, grated
⅔ cup oil
⅓ cup vinegar

1½ teaspoons tarragon
1 teaspoon salt
1½ tablespoons sugar
½ teaspoon dry mustard
½ clove garlic, crushed

Break lettuce into a bowl and add water chestnuts, sesame seeds and Parmesan cheese. Toss lightly. To make dressing, in a small bowl combine oil, vinegar, tarragon, salt, sugar, mustard and garlic. Mix well and pour as much as needed over salad; toss and taste. Serve at once. Serves four.

RYE PRETZELS

1 package dry yeast
1½ cups warm water
1 tablespoon malted milk powder
1 tablespoon molasses

1 teaspoon salt
4 to 4¾ cups rye flour
1 tablespoon caraway seeds
coarse salt

In mixing bowl, dissolve yeast in warm water. Add malted milk powder, molasses and salt. Stir in rye flour and caraway seeds. Knead till smooth, about 5 minutes. Cut into 12 portions; roll each to a rope 15 inches long. Shape into pretzels and place on a greased baking sheet. Moisten lightly with water and sprinkle with coarse salt. Bake in a 425-degree oven for 20 minutes or until browned. Makes 12 pretzels.

HAWAIIAN MIXED VEGETABLES
Carrots, mushrooms, water chestnuts and pineapple

2 tablespoons butter
5 large mushrooms, sliced
½ cup green pepper, coarsely chopped
1 cup onion, diced
1 cup pineapple chunks with juice
4 large carrots, diagonally sliced

⅛ teaspoon basil
¼ teaspoon ground ginger
⅛ teaspoon curry powder
1 tablespoon brown sugar
1 cup water chestnuts, drained and
  sliced

Melt butter in skillet, add mushrooms and sauté until golden. Add green pepper and sauté 3 minutes. Remove mushrooms and green pepper and set aside. In same skillet, add onions and cook until golden. Drain pineapple, reserving syrup. Add pineapple syrup, carrots, basil, ginger, curry powder and brown sugar to onions in skillet, and simmer 35 minutes or until carrots are tender. Add cooked mushrooms, green pepper, pineapple chunks and water chestnuts and cook 5 minutes longer. Serves four.

GARBANZO SNACKS

2 tablespoons butter
2 cloves garlic, crushed
1 cup dry garbanzo beans, cooked
1½ cups sesame seeds

½ teaspoon onion salt
¼ teaspoon dry mustard
½ teaspoon chili powder
1 teaspoon salt

Melt the butter in a heavy skillet, sauté the garlic, and then add the cooked garbanzos. Sauté slowly, stirring often, until garbanzos are golden brown and sizzling. They should be crunchy, but tender on the inside. Add remaining ingredients and blend. Eat hot if possible. Makes about 1½ cups.

HAWAIIAN HAUPIA
Coconut pudding

2 cups coconut milk
4 tablespoons sugar

5 tablespoons cornstarch
pinch of salt

Combine all ingredients in a saucepan. Cook over medium heat, stirring constantly until thickened. Pour into a pan and chill. Cut into squares to serve. Serves four.

CHEESE CAKE

2 cups cottage cheese
1 cup lemon yogurt
3 eggs, separated
1 teaspoon vanilla
1 tablespoon lemon juice

grated rind of one lemon
½ cup honey
¼ teaspoon salt
¼ cup wholewheat flour
graham cracker crust, 9-inch

Blend until smooth: cottage cheese, yogurt, egg yolks, vanilla, lemon juice and rind, honey, salt, and flour. Fold in stiffly beaten egg whites, and pour into a graham cracker crust. Bake in a moderate oven at 350 degrees, about 1 hour or until the center is firm. Delightful served with fresh berries.

FORTUNE COOKIES

¼ cup flour
2 tablespoons sugar
1 tablespoon cornstarch
dash of salt

2 tablespoons oil
1 egg white
1 tablespoon water

Write fortunes on 8 small slips of paper before starting to prepare the cookies. Sift together flour, sugar, cornstarch, and salt. Add oil and egg white; stir until smooth. Add water and mix well. Make one cookie at a time. Pour 1 tablespoon batter onto a lightly greased skillet or griddle, spreading batter to a 3½-inch circle. Cook over low heat for 4 minutes or until lightly browned. With wide spatula, lift and turn. Cook 1 minute longer. Working quickly, place cookie on pot holder or oven mitt. Put fortune in center; quickly fold cookie in half and curve folded edge over rim of mixing bowl to set. Place in muffin pan to cool. Makes 8 cookies.

HEALTHFUL FUDGE

1 cup honey
1 cup peanut butter
1 cup carob powder
1 cup shelled sunflower seeds

½ cup toasted sesame seeds
½ cup flaked coconut
½ cup walnuts, chopped
½ cup raisins

In large saucepan, heat honey and peanut butter, stirring constantly just until smooth. Remove from heat; stir in carob powder. Mix well. Add remaining ingredients. Press into buttered 8 × 8 × 2-inch pan. Chill several hours or overnight. Cut into 1-inch squares. Store in refrigerator. Makes 2¼ pounds of fudge.

DILL-ONION BREAD

1 cup cottage cheese
1 envelope dry yeast
¼ cup water
2 tablespoons sugar
1 tablespoon instant minced onion

1 tablespoon butter
2 teaspoons dill seed
¼ teaspoon soda
1 egg
2½ cups flour

Heat cottage cheese until warm. Combine with yeast, water, sugar, onion, butter, dill seed, soda and egg and flour; blend until smooth. Let rise about 1 hour or until doubled in bulk. Divide dough into two portions and place each in a tall one-pound coffee can. Let rise about 20 minutes or until can is three-fourths full. If dough rises too much, it will go over top of can during baking. Bake at 350 degrees for 40 minutes. Brush with melted butter when baked. Makes 2 loaves.

CHOCOLATE CHIP AND SUNFLOWER SEED COOKIES

½ cup soft butter
½ cup firmly packed brown sugar
1 egg
½ teaspoon vanilla
½ cup whole wheat flour
½ cup toasted wheat germ

½ teaspoon baking soda
½ teaspoon salt
1 package semisweet chocolate pieces,
   6 ounces
½ cup unsalted hulled sunflower seeds
½ cup shredded coconut

Cream together butter and sugar; add egg and vanilla and beat until fluffy. In another bowl, stir together the flour, wheat germ, soda and salt. Add to butter mixture and mix until blended. Stir in chocolate, sunflower seeds and coconut. Drop in rounded teaspoons about 2 inches apart on greased cookie sheets. Bake in a 350-degree oven for 10 to 12 minutes or until edges are lightly browned. With a wide spatula remove cookies to a rack to cool. Makes about 4 dozen.

Potpourri

Despite the enormous differences among the national cuisines, there is hardly a country that does not offer its own way of combining vegetables into a delicious main-dish meal. Many of these began with the peasant and farmer, who mixed together garden vegetables and herbs to create something wonderful. These people blended what was on hand, perhaps some beans or a few potatoes, a little green pepper, tomato or eggplant, and they seasoned with the herbs of the area, sometimes adding onion, garlic and oil, or a dash of red wine. Eggplant—both nutritious and versatile, and often called the "poor man's meat"—sometimes added its hearty touch. These vegetable stews not only changed personality from country to country, but often varied within one region of a country as well. Need and circumstance inspired many amazing recipes. Of course the good cook never slavishly adheres to specified measurements or ingredients in the preparation of a dish. For cooking can be an art, and art requires self-expression and imagination. In cooking the food of any country, the seasonings especially must be adjusted and adapted to taste.

POTPOURRI

ARROZ CON SALSA
Brazilian brown rice with sauce

Rice:

1 onion, chopped
3 cloves garlic, minced
2 tablespoons olive oil
2 tablespoons butter

2 tomatoes, peeled and coarsely chopped
2 cups brown rice, cooked

Sauté the onion and garlic in the olive oil and butter until the onion is golden. Add the tomatoes and simmer a few minutes. Stir in the cooked rice and keep warm over low heat while you make the sauce.

Sauce:

1 cup lemon juice
1 small onion, finely chopped
2 cloves garlic, finely chopped

1 tomato, peeled and finely diced
¼ cup canned green chilies, diced

Blend all ingredients in a blender until smooth or mix all ingredients thoroughly and serve over rice. Serves four.

BROWN SODA BREAD
Irish wheat and raisin bread

3 cups whole wheat flour
1 cup white flour
1 tablespoon baking powder
4 tablespoons sugar
1 teaspoon salt
½ cup butter

2 cups dark raisins
1⅓ cups buttermilk
1 egg
1 teaspoon baking soda
1 egg yolk plus 1 tablespoon water

In a bowl combine flour, baking powder, sugar and salt. With a pastry blender, cut in butter until mixture resembles cornmeal. Stir in raisins. Combine buttermilk, egg and baking soda in a small bowl until thoroughly blended. Stir buttermilk mixture into dry ingredients until well blended. Turn out onto a lightly floured board and knead lightly about 3 minutes or until dough is smooth. Form the dough into a 7-inch round on a lightly buttered baking sheet. With a sharp knife cut a cross about ½ inch deep into the top of the dough. Beat egg yolk and water together and brush mixture over top of dough. Bake the bread in a preheated oven at 375 degrees for 1 hour, or until it is golden brown. Transfer the bread to a rack and let it cool for 20 minutes before slicing. Makes 1 loaf.

MADURO EN GLORIA
Nicaraguan bananas cooked with cream cheese

4 tablespoons butter
6 firm bananas
¼ pound cream cheese

4 tablespoons sugar
1 teaspoon cinnamon
1 cup heavy cream

Melt the butter in a skillet. Peel the bananas and slice each one lengthwise. Brown quickly in the butter over high heat. Place half of the banana slices on the bottom of a buttered pie plate. Cream the cream cheese until very soft. Add the sugar and cinnamon, beating until light and smooth. Spread half of the mixture on the bananas. Place the remaining banana slices on top, then spread with the remainder of the cream cheese mixture. Pour the cream over the top. Bake in a 375-degree oven for 20 minutes, or until almost all the cream is absorbed and the top is lightly browned. Do not allow all the cream to be absorbed, or the bananas will be too dry. Serve hot. If desired, some whipped cream may be served with the bananas. Serves four.

ENGLISH ZUCCHINI-RICE CUSTARD

2 pounds zucchini
butter to coat dish
¾ cup minced parsley
3 tablespoons raw rice

salt and pepper
¾ cup flour
3 eggs
2½ cups milk

Wash, trim and cut the zucchini into ¼-inch slices. Arrange half the slices in a buttered 8 × 12-inch baking dish. Sprinkle the zucchini with parsley, and raw rice; season the mixture with salt and pepper. Shake the remaining zucchini in a paper bag containing flour, ½ teaspoon salt and ¼ teaspoon pepper; arrange zucchini over rice and parsley layer. Lightly beat eggs in a bowl and add milk and ½ teaspoon salt. Pour the mixture over the zucchini so that all the zucchini is well moistened. Bake the mixture in a preheated oven at 400 degrees, for 1½ hours, or until it is well browned. The custard may be served hot or at room temperature. Serves four.

TOMATO SWISS FONDUE

2 cups tomato juice
1 clove garlic
1 pound Swiss cheese, shredded
3 tablespoons cornstarch

¾ teaspoons salt
½ teaspoon Worcestershire
½ teaspoon crushed basil leaves
chunks of crisp French bread

In top of double boiler, heat 1¾ cups tomato juice with garlic until very hot. Place over boiling water and remove garlic. Add cheese, a small amount at a time, stirring constantly, until cheese is melted. At this point cheese may not be thoroughly combined with tomato juice. Combine cornstarch, salt, Worcestershire sauce and basil with ¼ cup tomato juice. Stir into cheese mixture. After cornstarch is added, cheese will combine with tomato juice for a smooth blend. Continue beating until smooth. If fondue becomes too thick, stir in a little more tomato juice. Serve from chafing dish or casserole over warmer, each person dipping chunks of bread into the fondue. For an interesting variation, in place of tomato juice, substitute white grape juice and omit basil leaves.

POCA
Turkish pastry balls filled with cheese

1 egg
1 cup yogurt
2 tablespoons olive oil
1 cup butter, melted
4 cups flour
1 teaspoon salt
1½ teaspoons baking powder

¾ cup farmer cheese or other soft
  white cheese
3 tablespoons chives, chopped
1½ tablespoons parsley, chopped
dash of salt and freshly ground pepper
4 tablespoons milk

To make the pastry, combine the egg, yogurt, olive oil and melted butter; beat with a whisk until well blended. Add the flour, salt and baking powder; stir to form a smooth dough. Cover and refrigerate for 15 minutes. In another bowl, combine the cheese, chives, parsley and a dash of salt and pepper. Roll a piece of dough the size of a walnut into a smooth ball. Press a finger into ball of dough and fill the hollow with ½ teaspoon of cheese mixture. Seal the dough around the filling and form into a ball again. Continue until all the dough is used. Butter a cookie sheet and place the cheese balls on the sheet. Brush each with milk. Bake in a preheated oven at 400 degrees, for 20 to 25 minutes. Serve warm. Will serve 8 or 10 as hors d'oeuvres.

FRUKTOVA SALATA
Bulgarian brandied fruit salad

3 apples
3 pears
2 oranges
1 cup pitted cherries

1 cup melon balls
½ cup honey
2 cups white wine
½ cup brandy

Peel and thinly slice the apples, pears and oranges and place in a bowl. Add cherries and melon balls. Over the fruit, pour honey and a mixture of the wine and brandy. Mix gently but thoroughly. Chill for at least 3 hours. Serve very cold. Serves four.

Index

SOUPS

VEGETABLE DISHES